he City of

STINE, FLA.

the United States.
re for Leon ist 1512,7

885.

RRIS, WELLGE & SWIFT, BROCKTON, MASS.

Institute of Classical Architecture & Art
20 West 44th Street, Suite 310, New York, NY 10036
Telephone: (212) 730-9646 Facsimile: (212) 730-9649
www.classicist.org

Russell Windham, Chairman
Peter Lyden, President
Classicist Committee of the ICAA:
Anne Kriken Mann and Gary Brewer, Co-Chairs;
Michael Mesko, David Rau, David Rinehart, William Rutledge, Suzanne Santry
Guest Editor: Elizabeth Plater-Zyberk

Managing Editor: Stephanie Salomon
Design: Suzanne Ketchoyian

ACKNOWLEDGMENTS

The ICAA, the *Classicist* Committee, and the Guest Editor would like to thank Steven Brooke for his stunning photography featured in *Classicist* No. 17, which includes the front and back covers as well as numerous images located throughout this issue. We are grateful for the contributions of all of the essay writers and their dedicated efforts on our behalf, as well as the anonymous peer reviewers to whom we owe special thanks. In Florida, Victor Deupi, Beth Dunlop (whose statewide knowledge was critical), Jorge Hernandez, Fletcher Isacks, Richard John, Joanna Lombard, Rick Lopez, Scott Merrill, Geoffrey Mouen, Katherine Pasternack, Ramon Trias (Planning Director, City of Coral Gables), Teofilo Victoria and the ICAA Florida Chapter, and—at DPZ CoDesign—Andres Duany, Xavier Iglesias, and Shannon Tracy, all provided advice and assistance. We also wish to acknowledge the scholarship and support of Robert A.M. Stern, whose keen eyes and encyclopedic mind are often called upon for reference. And, as always, we would like to thank the ICAA staff, particularly Mimi Bradley, without whom the *Classicist* would not become a reality.

PHOTO CREDITS

Front cover: Casino at Vizcaya, Miami, Florida, 1914–23, Francis Burrall Hoffman, Paul Chalfin, Diego Suarez. Photo: © Steven Brooke

Back cover: Detail of El Jardin, Miami, Florida, 1918, Kiehnel & Elliott. Photo: © Steven Brooke

Endpapers: Front: Bird's-eye view of Key West, Florida. Library of Congress Geography and Map Division Washington, D.C. Back: Bird's-eye View of St. Augustine, 1885. State Library of Florida, Florida Map Collection

Inventing an Architecture for Florida: Page 47: From *Coral Gables Design Best Practices,* 2016 (Arva Moore Parks Collection). Page 48: Top: © Steve Minor. Lower Left: Carol M. Highsmith Archive, Prints and Photographs Division,

Library of Congress. Lower Right: © Steven Richman. Page 49: Upper Left: Nikreates/Alamy Stock Photo. Upper Right: Ian Dagnall/Alamy Stock Photo. Bottom: © Steven Brooke. Page 50: Top: Courtesy of the State Archives of Florida. Lower Left and Lower Right: © Steven Brooke. Page 51: Upper Left, Middle, Lower Left, Lower Right, © Steven Brooke. Upper Right: Michael Mesko. Page 52: Upper Left: © Steven Brooke. Upper Right: Michael Mesko. Bottom: © Steve Minor. Page 53: Upper Left, Middle, Lower Left: © Steven Brooke. Right (top to bottom): 1, 2, 4 © Steve Minor; 3 and 5: © Steven Brooke. Page 54: Top: America/Alamy Stock Photo. Middle Left: Ebyabe/CC BY-SA 3.0. Middle Right, Lower Left, Lower Right: © Steven Brooke. Page 55: Upper Left: Courtesy of Fairfax, Sammons & Partners.

Upper Right, Middle Left, Middle Right, Bottom: © Steven Brooke. Page 56: Upper Left and Middle Left: Tim Arruda. Upper Right: Brian Jannsen/Alamy Stock Photo. Bottom: Museum of Fine Arts, St. Petersburg. Page 57: Top and Middle Left: © Steven Brooke. Middle Right: Glenn Darling. Bottom: Dick Dickinson, Dickinson Studios

Pages 65 and 83: Via Mizner, Palm Beach, Florida, 1923, Addison Mizner. Photos: © Steven Brooke

Page 99: The Kampong, National Tropical Botanical Garden, Coconut Grove, Florida, founded 1916 by David Fairchild. Photo: © Steven Brooke

Page 101: Gardens at Vizcaya, Miami, Florida, Photo: © Steven Brooke

Printing: Allied Printing Services, Manchester, CT

CLASSICIST № 17
FLORIDA

CORAL GABLES
Miami Riviera
40 Miles of Water Front
GEORGE E. MERRICK

LETTER FROM THE EDITOR

This issue of the *Classicist* presents a tour d'horizon of traditional architecture and urbanism in Florida. The earliest classical buildings began to appear in the mid-to-late nineteenth century in the north and central parts of the state, and represented the aspirations of new settlements. Essayist Bruce Stephenson describes the American Renaissance-era founding of Rollins College in Winter Park; Leslee Keys recounts Carrère & Hastings's resort creation in St. Augustine; and Wayne Wood reports on Henry John Klutho's role in the rebuilding of Jacksonville after a catastrophic fire.

The southern part of the state followed at the onset of the twentieth century. Beth Dunlop looks at Addison Mizner in Palm Beach; my own essay expands the picture to include Miami and Coral Gables, as well as more recent work; and the photographic essay illustrates other significant buildings. The land boom of the 1920s prompted a quick sequence of architecture, from Classical Revival to Mediterranean Revival to Art Deco. This lineage can be seen in the Professional Portfolio, showing a rich range of application, from revival orthodoxy to inventive interpretations.

Classicical principles deployed in a formal revival of Renaissance, Roman, and Greek precedents were reserved most often for buildings of civic importance. For the everyday functions of residence and commerce, the informal vernacular became preferred. The accommodating character of the picturesque Mediterranean is evident in construction details that betray the speed and quantity of speculative building. And there is wisdom in its acknowledgment of the tropical context—the limits to materials available at the far end of the peninsula, the unmerciful assault of the elements, and the production methods required by a booming market.

The clarity of this conceptual duality—the classical as monumental and civic, and the Mediterranean as suited to the urban fabric—came into focus in a pattern that informed three decades of intense urban growth in the state before ceding to the influence of the International style in the 1930s. That transition, too, is interesting for its distinct regional character. Architects trained in Beaux-Arts techniques combined the formal symmetry of Classical Revival with the picturesque massing of Mediterranean Revival to produce a new form of building, embellished with a high degree of relief advantaged in the tropical sun. These colorful and joyful buildings remain intact in the Art Deco District of Miami Beach.

Can contemporary social, health, and climate concerns be enlightened by such architectural precedent? Indeed! Buildings and urbanism tell us of the aspirations of our predecessors, and how we came to be in this place. They can also teach us about still-useful place-based experience.

Florida's early twentieth-century city founders sought an environment of good health, following years of war and influenza. Buildings emphasized outdoor living with generous porches, loggias, and courtyards. Arcades protected sidewalks from sunlight and downpours. Lessons also can be found in the historic interchangeability of land and water—canals excavated and islands filled—as we seek to respond to a shrinking footprint of dry land.

Still to be reckoned with is Florida's social history, which followed the example of the South. The African American and Caribbean builders who turned the visions of new cities into reality were burdened for many years by segregation and limits on wealth generation. What today some find inspiring, others see as troubling markers.

As these challenges evolve, our peninsular history and its architecture remind us of the durability and transcendence of classicism's humanist principles. Suspended between the admired work of predecessors and a future still to be written, we can strive for a perspective broad enough to enable the past to inspire the future.

—Elizabeth Plater-Zyberk, Guest Editor

Denman Fink, 1926 advertising illustration for Coral Gables, showing the Venetian Pool by architect Phineas Paist and artist Denman Fink, completed 1924.

PALACES IN PARADISE

CARRÈRE & HASTINGS IN ST. AUGUSTINE

LESLEE F. KEYS

*Carrère & Hastings were now the unchallenged overseers of the largest and
most unusual building project under way in the United States, subject only to the phantasmal vision
and inexhaustible pocketbook of Henry Morrison Flagler.*
—William Morrison

In 1885, young New York architects John Merven Carrère and Thomas Hastings received their inaugural architectural commission: a contract with Henry Morrison Flagler to design his first Florida resort, the Hotel Ponce de Leon in St. Augustine. A co-founder of Standard Oil with John D. Rockefeller, Flagler was a partner with ten other northern businessmen in the Plant Investment Company (PICO), established to develop the southernmost frontier of the United States—the Florida peninsula stretching south from Orlando.[1]

SPANISH ST. AUGUSTINE

Flagler had become enamored with St. Augustine beginning with his winter visit of 1883, returning each of the following two winters. Founded by the Spanish in 1565, St. Augustine is the oldest continuously inhabited European settlement in the contiguous United States and features the nation's earliest example of a planned city, designed in accordance with the 1573 Laws of the Indies. The city was platted one mile in length along the banks of the Matanzas River and one-half mile in width west from the river with the Plaza (de la Constitución) as the central feature. Anchoring the northern boundary is the Castillo de San Marcos (1672–95), the nation's only seventeenth-century fortification, designed on a plan derived from Spanish engineer Bautista Antonelli. The St. Francis [of Assisi] Barracks, built by friars between 1724 and 1755 (and since 1907, the headquarters of the Florida National Guard), marks the southern boundary.

At the time, the city's western boundary was Maria Sanchez Creek, ultimately the setting for three Flagler buildings designed by Carrère & Hastings. The first of those buildings, the Hotel Ponce de Leon, afforded exceptional views of the city then and now. The Cathedral Basilica and Trinity Episcopal Church face the Plaza, as does the former Customs House and Post Office. Most buildings in the city are small, and a height limitation of thirty-five feet, adopted in 1963, ensures that the city's iconic skyline is preserved.

Named for the Spanish explorer Juan Ponce de León, the Hotel Ponce de Leon was a palatial Spanish Renaissance Revival structure that paid homage to palaces and cathedrals of Spain's Golden Age that today are World Heritage Sites. In 1968, the hotel became the centerpiece of the newly founded Flagler College (fig. 1). The Ponce, as it had been known throughout its history, remains as Carrère & Hastings's most creative endeavor and ranks as the single property listed as a National Historic Landmark for its association with the architects.

Carrère & Hastings designed several structures in St. Augustine for Flagler: Grace [United] Methodist Church (1886–87), the Hotel Alcazar (Lightner Museum) (1887–89), and Flagler Memorial Presbyterian Church (1889–90), which includes the Flagler family mausoleum (1906) and Flagler's residence, Kirkside (1893, demolished 1950). Architectural historians Laurie Ossman and Heather Ewing have referred to the collection as a "stunningly ambitious architectural ensemble."[2]

Fig. 1. Detail of Hotel Ponce de Leon (today the cornerstone of Flagler College), St. Augustine, 1885–87, by Carrère & Hastings.

Also, Flagler engaged the architects for projects in Palm Beach. Architect C. Channing Blake and historian Susan Braden have acknowledged that "an unnamed project in Palm Beach in 1893" by Carrère & Hastings may have been the Beaux Arts Hotel Royal Poinciana (1894). The architects designed Whitehall (1900-1902), Flagler's palatial marble winter home. In 1959–60, his youngest granddaughter, Jean Flagler Matthews, restored the Gilded Age mansion known today as the Henry Morrison Flagler Museum (see p. 41, fig. 3).[3]

Flagler's selection of Carrère & Hastings reinforced existing family relationships and friendships. Flagler and Hastings were cousins, sharing the same great-great grandfather. The duo graduated from the Ecole des Beaux-Arts, and the architects enlisted their former École roommates Emmanuel Masqueray and Bernard Maybeck, each of whom became successful in his own right. Maybeck reunited with Hastings in 1915, generating his most famous work, the Palace of Fine Arts for San Francisco's Panama-Pacific International Exposition.[4]

Addressing the partners' careers, Blake commends their efforts in the design and construction of a complex project: "First, Carrère and Hastings asserted themselves as the vanguard of American monumental planning...The Ponce de Leon Hotel, in particular, revealed their mastery of the arrangement of large spaces and building blocks that surpassed all other efforts in the second half of the 1880's. Second, they evidenced real invention and competence in the technical problems of monolithic concrete construction long before their contemporaries began to consider the structural possibilities inherent in the material...Third, Carrère and Hastings demonstrated that they were extremely proficient in the vocabulary of the Renaissance style and quick to adapt that style to American conditions and materials."[5]

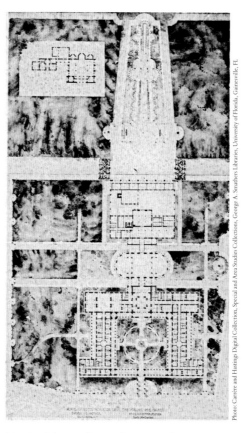

Fig 2. Plans of Hotel Ponce de Leon, a proposed Cascade for the property, and [inset] of Grace M[ethodist] E[piscopal] Church (built east of proposed Cascade), St. Augustine, 1885–87, by Carrère & Hastings.

Photo: Carrère and Hastings Digital Collection, Special and Area Studies Collections, George A. Smathers Libraries, University of Florida, Gainesville, FL

THE HOTEL PONCE DE LEON

A five-building, 270,000-square-foot, linear complex, the Ponce was constructed on the eastern portion of a square, six-acre parcel of land immediately west of the city. The western portion of the parcel included gardens and recreational areas. Four stories of guest rooms framed the entrance to the hotel, which was through a large square courtyard that led into the Rotunda. Inside, perpendicular hallways provided access to the Grand Parlor or guest services, or to a magnificent staircase that led to the Dining Room. Beyond the latter were the kitchen and hotel staff facilities. The Edison Boiler Building, which housed the steam dynamo powering the hotel, and the Artists' Studios, a series of seven ateliers for guest artists, completed the Ponce compound (fig. 2).

Work on the 450-room complex took eighteen months and was completed in May of 1887, though the winter resort did not open until January 1888. Carrère & Hastings oversaw materials, techniques, and processes for the $2.5 million project (the equivalent of nearly $70 million today). Hastings is credited with details on the exterior and interior.

The design reflected a variety of Spanish buildings. Seville's Alcázar palace is represented through the strength and solidity of the Ponce's composition, and the Seville Cathedral's Giralda bell tower, a minaret from a former mosque with a Renaissance spire, is evident in the Ponce's two 165-foot-tall towers. The Aljaferia Palace in Zaragoza exerted influence through the use of brick and stone construction. Elaborate patterns and shell motifs were adopted from the University of Salamanca, and the patterned tower roofs were adapted from the churches of San Martín and San Esteban in Segovia. Inspiration for the courtyards, fountains, and loggias came from the Alhambra in Granada.

Along with innovative design, the Ponce featured the use of pioneer-

Fig. 3. Hotel Ponce de Leon, entry courtyard and front facade illustrating a polychromatic scheme featuring poured concrete, brick, and terra-cotta materials.

ing construction materials. The unreinforced poured concrete walls incorporated St. Augustine's native coquina-shell stone, using equal parts of sand and concrete and double that amount of coquina. The walls varied from four feet thick in the basement to 16–20 inches thick for the upper stories. Baetjer and Meyerstein of New York imported the mortar from Hanover, Germany, supplying 50,000 barrels for the Ponce, and later, the same quantities were used for the Hotel Alcazar and Hotel Cordova.

Contrasting with the rhythmic horizontal bands of the pearl-gray walls, the red bricks with matching mortar and the red clay-tinted terra-cotta provided a dramatic polychromatic effect. Additionally, the exuberant combination of balconies, alcoves, loggias, and arcades and 1,000 windows brought the scale of the building to one that visitors could enjoy (fig. 3).

The project team reflected innovations of the time. Former shipbuilders James McGuire and Joseph McDonald oversaw the Ponce's construction with assistance from engineer William Kennish. Simultaneously,

Kennish served as the chief inspector for the erection of the base of the Statue of Liberty. Thomas Edison's direct-current electricity facilitated power and more than 4,000 lights. Louis Comfort Tiffany, in the beginning of his glassmaking career, and with assistance from glass artist Maitland Armstrong, created designs for the building's seventy-nine stained-glass windows. They remain as the largest collection of stained-glass windows in the world in their original location (fig. 4).

George Willoughby Maynard, considered the nation's foremost muralist at the time, conceived the allegorical figures painted on the ceilings of the Rotunda and Dining Room. Virgilio Tojetti created murals on canvas in Paris that were installed in the four quadrants of the Grand Parlor. Prior to the construction of New York's skyscrapers, his works could be appreciated in many small New York hotels and mansions. Today, the collection of four in the Ponce remain as rare extant examples of his work.

The interior of the building reflects the New World's Spanish heritage and intersperses Victorian cherubs, lions, and sea serpents as playful contrast. The Rotunda's

Fig. 4. Hotel Ponce de Leon, Dining Room featuring stained glass by Louis Comfort Tiffany.

Fig. 5. Hotel Ponce de Leon, Rotunda, with ceiling murals, four of which were reproduced for the Library of Congress.

ceiling arches feature names of explorers, including Pánfilo de Narváez, Hernando de Soto, and Juan Ponce de León. Provincial coats-of-arms are highlighted—among them those representing Cádiz, València, Vizcaya, Málaga, Castellón, and Barcelona (figs. 4, 5).

The ceiling in the Grand Parlor's main salon honors the year 1512. King Ferdinand authorized Juan Ponce de León's voyage that November. His efforts resulted in the exploration of "La Florida," where he landed in April 1513. Encircling the ceiling in the main salon and in the Rotunda are conquistadors' helmets cast in plaster.

The Rotunda structure extends upward to support the central dome at the top of the building. In the summer of 1886, during the hotel's construction, St. Augustine witnessed three hurricanes. Those events may have figured in Flagler's decision to have the dome and its flanking towers reinforced with track from his Florida East Coast Railway. In 2015, the Solarium, the room immediately under the dome, was the setting for an event with dignitaries from Spain and the United States honoring Their Majesties King Felipe VI and Queen Letizia of Spain.

Immediately southeast of the Ponce is the Hotel Cordova (1885–88), now the Casa Monica Hotel, which was designed by Bostonian Franklin W. Smith, who pioneered the use of poured concrete in St. Augustine. Flagler funded the hotel and acquired it at the end of its first season.

THE HOTEL ALCAZAR

Shortly after construction began on the Ponce, Flagler enlisted Carrère & Hastings to conceive a second hotel across the arterial King Street to the south, the Hotel Alcazar. According to Ossman and Ewing, this decision enabled the architectural team to introduce Beaux-Arts city planning principles. "The Alcazar was the crucial counterpoint to the Ponce de Léon" in this scheme. The elaborate courtyards and the Alameda Gardens in front of the Alcazar linked the hotels visually and softened the appearance of the massive concrete and terra-cotta structures, inviting visitors to stroll among them.[6]

Achieving this design ensemble necessitated removal of the Methodist church that occupied the future Alcazar site. Flagler underwrote a new Methodist church to be built one block north of the Ponce. Carrère & Hastings designed Grace United Methodist Church (1886–87) and its parsonage in the Spanish Renaissance Revival style and repeated the use of poured concrete with brick and terra-cotta detailing at a cost of $85,000 (fig. 6).

The Hotel Alcazar (1887–89), executed in poured concrete, presents a commanding fortress appearance

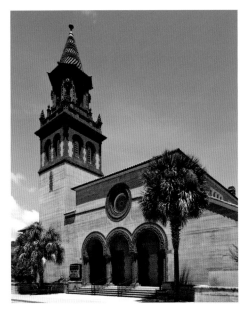

Fig. 6. Grace United Methodist Church, St. Augustine, 1886–87, by Carrère & Hastings.

Fig. 7. Hotel Alcazar (today the Lightner Museum), St. Augustine, 1887–89, by Carrère & Hastings.

befitting an edifice with a name that in Arabic means "house of Caesar." The building is a simplified interpretation of Rome's Villa Medici. Brick and terra-cotta minarets, lion details, chimneys, and delicate spires with finials draw the eyes of the viewer skyward. The two towers feature classical elements, including substantial belvederes framed with pairs of Corinthian columns shielding smaller Ionic columns. As built, the $1 million structure included 300 hotel rooms. The hotel quickly became popular, and in 1891, Flagler added a fourth floor (figs. 7, 8).[7]

"If the Ponce de Leon charmed, the Alcazar... delighted," Susan Braden has noted. Also arranged in a linear design, the rear section of the Alcazar housed activity and amusement spaces for guests. Turkish and Russian baths, Swedish massage rooms, parlors, game rooms, a gymnasium, and a ballroom were included. The most significant feature was a 156-foot swimming pool, complete with dressing rooms. In addition, the property included tennis courts, visible from the south entrance.[8]

Fig. 8. Detail of Hotel Alcazar tower.

FLAGLER MEMORIAL PRESBYTERIAN CHURCH AND MAUSOLEUM

In mid-April 1889, shortly after the season's closing of Flagler's hotels, construction began on a Carrère & Hastings project that Flagler had envisioned for several years—a Presbyterian church to be located diagonally northwest of the Ponce. The implementation and accelerated schedule of the project reflected, in part, his interest in honoring his daughter Jennie Louise Benedict, who had died the month before from complications associated with childbirth.

Designed in the Venetian Renaissance Revival style, the cruciform-shaped building was topped with a copper-plated dome that rose to a height of 150 feet and was completed with a 20-foot-tall Greek cross. Featuring elements of Spanish, Baroque, Moorish, and Roman architecture, the style is unique in that the spires atop the two towers were executed in white terra-cotta. The poured-concrete walls were reinforced, as were the final sections of the Ponce, with Flagler's Florida East Coast Railway track (fig. 9).[9]

Fig. 9. Flagler Memorial Presbyterian Church, 1889, and Mausoleum, 1906, St. Augustine, by Carrère & Hastings.

Among the elaborate interior details is a carved shell hewn from a single piece of mahogany approximately six feet in diameter, which is suspended over the pulpit. Several stained-glass windows, representing Christian religious beliefs and created by artisan Herman Schladermundt, were installed in 1901–2.[10]

The Manse (or Church House), immediately north and part of the same parcel of land, was designed in the same style. On March 16, 1890, the first anniversary of Jennie Louise Benedict's death, Flagler Memorial Presbyterian Church was dedicated.[11]

In 1906, Flagler commissioned Carrère & Hastings for one final work in St. Augustine. The architects designed the domed Flagler Mausoleum in a Colonial Revival style and constructed it on the west side of the sanctuary. In 1911, with construction completed, Flagler had the graves of his first wife, Mary Harkness Flagler, his daughter Jennie Louise Benedict, and his granddaughter Margery Benedict reinterred there. In May 1913, Henry Morrison Flagler's was the final burial in the tomb.

Flagler's vision for St. Augustine included bringing the railroad to the city and building the station west of town near the banks of the San Sebastian River. He supported reconstruction of the fire-damaged Catholic Church and construction of the Ancient City Baptist Church. His enterprises constructed the Alicia Hospital, the YMCA, the *St. Augustine Record* newspaper building, City Hall, and the City Ice and Fuel Company. He provided land for the St. Augustine Water Works Pumping Station. The Flagler Model Land Company developed residences north of the hotels. In addition, Flagler introduced golf to Florida, sponsored the Cuban Giants Negro League Baseball Team, hosted collegiate and professional tennis and swimming, improved streets, and established parks. He was a lifetime member of the St. Augustine Yacht Club. Carrère & Hastings were integral to the success of his vision.

CARRÈRE & HASTINGS'S ST. AUGUSTINE LEGACY

John Carrère and Thomas Hastings recognized the strategic importance of their first commission. Carrère commented on St. Augustine's individuality and European charm. Hastings noted the significance of retaining the city's quaintness and Spanish character. As had their patron Henry Flagler, both men enjoyed the "ancient city" and returned to St. Augustine throughout their lives.[12]

St. Augustine's picturesque skyline showcases Carrère & Hastings's efforts. Their designs and city planning concepts remain protected and preserved as major highlights of St. Augustine's Spanish heritage and internationally as unique representations of their time.

At its opening, the Hotel Ponce de Leon was hailed as the world's most luxurious and modern hotel. In 1957, for the American Institute of Architects' centennial anniversary, the organization recognized the seventy-year-old Ponce as one of the "100 Most Important Buildings" in the nation. Early in its history, Flagler College committed to preserving the former hotel and nearby buildings associated with Henry Flagler, comprising fourteen buildings in addition to the five buildings of the Ponce. Today, the campus is recognized as one of the most beautiful college settings in the nation and the world.

Throughout their careers, John Carrère and Thomas Hastings designed more than 600 buildings, making their firm one of the most prolific of the age. Carrère died in 1911, shortly before the opening of their monumental New York Public Library. Hastings continued the architectural practice under the firm name until his death in 1929. Highlights of that era illustrate skills he honed with Carrère in St. Augustine, notably his 1914 design for the Casa de los Marqueses de Avilés in Havana, Cuba.[13]

The influence of Carrère & Hastings's work in Florida inspired architecture in the United States for half a century. Ossman and Ewing express it aptly. "St. Augustine made their careers, and while the society visitors moved on, the impact of the work reverberated through the American architectural scene for the next four decades."[14]

Dr. Leslee F. Keys is Director of Historic Preservation and Assistant Professor of History at Flagler College in St. Augustine. She serves as the college's historic preservation expert and oversees the fine and decorative arts collection. Her book, *Hotel Ponce de Leon: The Rise, Fall, and Rebirth of Flagler's Gilded Age Palace* (University Press of Florida, 2015), received a 2016 William L. Proctor Award. She is the 2015 inaugural recipient of the Florida Trust for Historic Preservation's Roy E. Graham Award for Excellence in Historic Preservation Education and the 2016 inaugural recipient of the University of Florida's Distinguished Alumni Award in Historic Preservation.

Notes

1. (Epigraph) William Morrison, quoted in Laurie Ossman, "Carrère and Hastings," presentation at Flagler College, May 21, 2006. Mark Hewitt, et al., *Carrère and Hastings: Architects* (New York: Acanthus Press, 2006), 63. Leslee F. Keys, *Hotel Ponce de Leon: The Rise, Fall, and Rebirth of Flagler's Gilded Age Palace* (Gainesville, FL: University Press of Florida, 2015), 11–13.

2. Laurie Ossman and Heather Ewing, *Carrère and Hastings: The Masterworks* (New York: Rizzoli International Publications, 2011), 38

3. Curtis Channing Blake, "The Architecture of Carrère and Hastings" (PhD diss., Columbia University, 1976), 391. Susan Braden, *The Architecture of Leisure: The Florida Resort Hotels of Henry Flagler and Henry Plant* (Gainesville, FL: University Press of Florida, 2002), 210.

4. Laura A. Ackley, *San Francisco's Jewel City: The Panama-Pacific International Exposition of 1915* (Berkeley, CA: California Historical Society, 2015), 3. Esther McCoy, *Five California Architects.* (New York: Reinhold Book Corporation, 1960), 25.

5. Blake, "The Architecture of Carrère and Hastings," 99–100.

6. Ossman and Ewing, *Carrère and Hastings,* 38.

7. Braden, *The Architecture of Leisure,* 180.

8. Ibid., 178–182. National Park Service, "Hotel Ponce de Leon," National Historic Landmark Nomination, 2005. Ossman and Ewing, *Carrère and Hastings,* 42.

9. Jennie Louise Flagler Benedict was married to Frederick Hart Benedict. He was the brother of Helen Ripley Benedict, who married architect Thomas Hastings. Hastings's brother Frank Hastings, an executive with Edison's electric company, married a Benedict cousin. National Park Service, "Flagler Memorial Presbyterian Church," National Register of Historic Places Nomination, 1983.

10. Interview by the author with Jay Smith, Historian and Elder, Flagler Memorial Presbyterian Church, March 29, 2020.

11. National Park Service, "Flagler Memorial Presbyterian Church."

12. Thomas Graham, *Mr. Flagler's St. Augustine* (Gainesville, FL: University Press of Florida, 2014), 6.

13. Hastings's Havana design is home to the British Ambassador to Cuba. See Hermes Mallea, *Great Houses of Havana: A Century of Cuban Style* (New York: The Monacelli Press, 2011), 73.

14. Ossman and Ewing, *Carrère and Hastings,* 43.

ROLLINS COLLEGE AND WINTER PARK

EXEMPLARS OF THE AMERICAN RENAISSANCE

BRUCE STEPHENSON

In recent years, both *The Princeton Review* and *Condé Nast Traveler* named Rollins College one of the most beautiful campuses in the nation. The decisions were based on survey results, but the iconic beauty of Florida's oldest private college is rooted in history (fig. 1). Its harmonious blend of Mediterranean Revival architecture, intimate greens and plazas, scenic vistas, covered walkways, and oak-shaded paths is an exemplar of the American Renaissance, a generational effort to mold an unparalleled prosperity into a new urban civilization.

THE AMERICAN RENAISSANCE: THE EVOLUTION OF URBANISM

The movement began in the 1880s and disappeared after 1930, "the last full flourish of the Renaissance that began in Italy in the fifteenth century," Henry Hope Reed wrote.[1] By the 1890s, a "Renaissance complex," the sense of a culture that inspired receptiveness to beauty and humane concerns, had permeated artistic and intellectual circles in the United States.[2] Like their fifteenth-century predecessors, the Americans rejected doctrinaire religion. Darwin had turned orthodox belief into a faded, esoteric experience that failed to address the challenge of modern life—urbanization. The Industrial Revolution had initiated a rapid shift from country to city, a transformation that marked "the tensions in the struggle for existence," ethicist Edward Howard Griggs wrote in his seminal text, *The New Humanism* (1899).[3] In response, reformers embraced "environmentalism": the belief that societal evolution was determined by both individual character and living conditions. United in the conviction that humans were more good than evil, a cohort of Ivy League graduates established the city planning profession

Fig. 1. Walkway on the campus of Rollins College, Winter Park, Florida.

in the early twentieth century to direct progress to a higher plane by improving the health, beauty, and function of the city. This effort also proceeded in the midst of millennial change.[4] "The civilization characteristic of Christendom has not yet disappeared, yet another civilization has begun to take its place," philosopher George Santayana noted in 1913.[5]

John Nolen and Frederick Law Olmsted Jr. played central roles in the new profession. In 1905, Nolen earned one of the first master's degrees in landscape architecture from Harvard University, and joined the small cadre of reformers drafting the nation's first comprehensive city plans. Civic centers were the focal points. Designed with "dignity and appropriate beauty," they exerted, Nolen wrote, an "ennobling influence" that crystallized civic impulses into "action for the public good."[6] Park systems were included. Providing access to nature was a moral good, and a physical and mental imperative in a world set to the factory regimen. Integrating suburban neighborhoods into the expanding American city was the final component, and Frederick Law Olmsted Sr.'s Riverside, Illinois, set the standard.

Lying nine miles west of Chicago on a commuter rail spur, the idyllic community was designed to harbor "suburban yeomen" who tended gardens and lived close to nature. The floodplain of the Des Plaines River was enveloped in a park, a green backbone that ran roughly north to south through the community. At the park's juncture with the rail line, the town center was set on a grid. The rest of Riverside broke from the traditional grid arrangement, and its alignment with nature exemplified how "the arts of civilization," Olmsted wrote, could channel the "flood" of urbanization into humane form.[7]

WINTER PARK:
MODEL COMMUNITY

In 1881, the American Renaissance came to Central Florida when Chicago businessmen Loring Chase and Oliver Chapman purchased 600 acres along a rail line to build a model town. Mimicking Riverside, their 1883 town plan for Winter Park was a modified neoclassical grid with radiating concentric circles denoting five-minute walks from a train station in a central park. The town developed at a pedestrian scale and in a context-sensitive manner. A variety of building types, heights, and design approaches were employed, while civic institutions occupied key locations. Like Riverside, Winter Park's compact downtown was aligned on a principal street, Park Avenue, that paralleled a park. The downtown also blended with informal neighborhoods laid out in a parklike setting.

Culture and art were instilled in the town's milieu after Rollins College, founded by New Congregationalists and constituting Florida's first private institution of higher learning, opened in 1885. Sited between the downtown's southern terminus and Lake Virginia, the college raised civic awareness and set the intellectual foundation for a region on the edge of a frontier. The stripling liberal arts institution struggled, however, until the 1920s.[8] By then, the advent of middle-class tourism was transforming the state into the "Eden of the South," Lewis Mumford wrote, "the desire of the heart and the end of human aspirations."[9] In the midst of the greatest real estate boom in American history, Hamilton Holt accepted the presidency of Rollins, because, he stated in 1925, "Florida is the one state where the spirit of progress most prevails and where results follow quickest from effort."[10]

A consummate reformer, the longtime editor of *The Independent* wanted to break the staid academic formula by marrying pragmatism and the liberal arts. Setting out to direct Rollins College on an "adventure in common sense education," his first priority, Holt wrote to John Nolen, was building "an ideal campus."[11] Nolen had

Fig. 2. Hamilton Holt's master plan for Rollins College as designed by Richard Kiehnel of Miami, 1929.

drawn plans for Davidson College, the University of North Carolina, Queens College, and the University of Wisconsin, but it was his pathbreaking work in designing Florida new towns that excited Holt.

HAMILTON HOLT:
PRAGMATIC VISIONARY

Holt and Nolen were confidants, progressive stalwarts who had led a delegation that pleaded with President Woodrow Wilson not to go to war in early April 1917. "Think how the different the world would be if we had succeeded," Nolen wrote to Holt after they had reconnected in Florida.[12] The dreams of world peace that permeated the progressive mindset were long gone by the mid-1920s, but the two men took solace in the opportunities Florida offered.

"The story of Florida is a story of adventure and romance written through a long history—four centuries....The early search was for the Fountain of Youth and for gold, and the modern one is not essentially different," Nolen proclaimed at a 1925 city planning conference.[13] Flimflam and opportunism were rampant, but there was also significant investment in city building. By decade's end, Florida was the first former Confederate state to have a majority of its population classified as urban. During the 1920s, Nolen earned multiple commissions in the state he called "the nation's great laboratory of city planning."[14]

The aesthetic competence that imbued Nolen's new town of Venice marked the zenith of American town planning before the Great Depression.[15] "Nature led the way," Nolen wrote of his wide-ranging regional plan that melded farms, open space, neighborhoods, and mixed-use centers in a new type of suburbanism.[16] Venice Avenue ran through the center of a three-block commercial core and apartment-hotel district. Loggias were designed to line the street and provide shade. Where the Gulf of Mexico came into view, the avenue broadened into a

Fig. 3. Bird's-eye view of the Rollins College campus, laid out as a neo-Renaissance village.

parkway, and city hall was sited at this point. Planted with palms, live oaks, and subtropical vegetation, the parkway terminated at a beachfront preserve with an amphitheater. This assignment epitomized the neo-Renaissance plan's essence—classical motifs would elevate the modern mind by immersing a prosperous people in the outdoors and the arts. The Mediterranean Revival architecture did the same: the train station and the bank were inspired by two Venetian landmarks, the campanile in the Piazza San Marco and the Palazzo Ducale.[17]

Nolen's renaissance vision inspired Holt, as did the work of Nolen confidant George Merrick. A former Rollins student and the developer of Coral Gables, Merrick drew on Winter Park in his plan for the nascent Miami suburb that drew national attention for its unmatched assemblage of Mediterranean Revival architecture. Open courtyards, tiled roofs, stucco exteriors, high ceilings, and arched windows and doorways combined practicality and aesthetics to meet the challenge of Florida's hot, humid climate.[18] Holt spent a year examining Mediterranean Revival projects in Miami and St. Petersburg, and was especially impressed by the Rolyat Hotel designed by Richard Kiehnel.[19]

A German-born architect, Kiehnel was trained at the Ecole des Beaux-Arts and came to Miami in 1922. He earned a series of commissions in Coral Gables, but the Rolyat in St. Petersburg was his definitive work. The symmetrical harmony of the elegant series of structures that now house Stetson University College of Law was inspired by Seville's Torre del Oro. Holt wanted a similar statement, and he hired Kiehnel to design a campus plan. Like Venice, Rollins had an axial orientation with two key buildings (theater and chapel) set on a central square. The plan's focal point, however, was the library (fig. 2).[20]

Envisioned as a commanding twenty-nine-story structure, the library was the terminus for a central axis that bisected a linear green and a common lawn. Slated to be Florida's tallest building, the Rollins library paid homage to the University of Virginia and the iconic "academic village" planned by Thomas Jefferson. Jefferson placed the Rotunda, a half-size adaptation of the Pantheon housing the library, at the terminus of a linear lawn. The rounded cranium housed the "brain" of the university, and it faced an unbounded horizon to symbolize the flow of knowledge into the young republic.[21] Jefferson imagined a new kind of university dedicated to educating leaders in intellectual and practi-

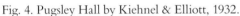

Fig. 4. Pugsley Hall by Kiehnel & Elliott, 1932.

Fig. 5. Loggia behind Mayflower Hall by Kiehnel & Elliott, 1930.

cal affairs and, a century later, this archetype infused the plan for Rollins.

Kiehnel grouped twenty-nine structures to form a neo-Renaissance academic village (fig. 3). Both Rollins College and the University of Virginia adopted the lessons of the Italian Renaissance, which emphasized a new, more engaged urban culture in which citizens spent much of their free time in public plazas and markets. Renaissance architect Leon Battista Alberti believed these public spaces helped divert young men and women from "the mischievousness and folly natural to their age," and the Rollins campus is a testament to this tradition.[22] Loggias, a staple of Florentine architecture, were paramount. Covered walkways linked the campus, while classrooms and dormitories were set on quadrangles and small court-yards to capture breezes and foster air circulation. "Breezy and cool" was how Holt described the scheme to create the first "open-air college" in the United States.[23] Finally, intimate greens and small squares offered places of repose to activate thought and offer an escape from the swirl of campus life. A model of compact urbanism, the campus

was built to a scale that respected the human form and celebrated intellectual inquiry.

Kiehnel was the architect for the first Rollins dormitories, Mayflower and Pugsley halls, sited in conjunction with the campus plan. Opening in 1932, Pugsley Hall marked the terminus of Park Avenue, which Kiehnel celebrated with an artistically detailed entrance of Florida traver-tine stone with engaged composite columns framing an ornate iron gate. A tiled barrel roof, stone trimmings, iron-grilled windows, and wood balconies exemplified the Spanish Mediterranean style that Mayflower Hall replicated (fig. 4). Cypress-beam ceilings with colored ornamentation highlighted the interiors, and the build-ings were joined by a second-story loggia with large arches resting on massive columns. The two residences were later connected by a common first-floor loggia running along the back of the structures that front Holt Avenue on the northern end of campus[24] (fig. 5).

The library was never built to the plan's outsized specifi-cations. In fact, funding for what would be named Mills Library was not secured until 1949, the year Holt retired.

Fig. 6. Knowles Memorial Chapel by Ralph Cram and Annie Russell Theatre by Kiehnel & Elliott, 1932.

Designed by James Gamble Rogers II, the two-story steel-framed stucco building had a commanding arched entryway. From its steps, one could glean a picturesque view that extended into Winter Park, as the oaks framing Interlachen Avenue directed the eye to the horizon. The axis running from Mills Library north into Winter Park was the also path students took to complete their graduation ceremony. They marched across Mills Lawn to the Congregational Church on Interlachen, where they were introduced to the community as citizens ready for service.

The campus showpieces were the Knowles Memorial Chapel and the Annie Russell Theatre (1932), now listed on the National Register of Historic Places (fig. 6). Ralph Cram, a noted ecclesiastical architect, designed Knowles Chapel, while Kiehnel drew the plans for the Annie Russell.

Cram designed more than seventy-five churches and cathedrals in both the United States and Europe. The celebrated Cathedral of St. John the Divine in New York City and the chapels at West Point and Princeton University were built in the refined neo-Gothic style Cram championed. After studying Spanish-style late

Renaissance cathedrals, he returned to the United States, "fired up aesthetically and spiritually."[25] Seventeenth-century Spanish architecture intrigued Cram, representing a period when Renaissance fashion transitioned to more classical forms, "but," he noted, "before the Spanish builders had gone to the lengths of elaboration found in the churches of Mexico."[26] He modeled Knowles Chapel's towering campanile on the Toledo Cathedral. Special care was given to a tympanum carved in stone above the front entrance that illustrates Florida's unique history. Designed by William F. Ross of Cambridge, Massachusetts, and carved by Ardolino of New York, it depicts Franciscan friars, flanked by Spanish conquistadors and Native people, planting the first cross in American soil.[27] The message aligned with the college's founding mission that devout Congregationalists enunciated to "provide students with the best educational facilities possible and to throw about them those Christian influences, which will be adopted to restrain them from evil and prepare them for a virtuous, happy and useful life."[28]

When the chapel opened in 1932, Rollins was a much more secular institution. Chapel attendance was no longer mandatory, but thought and reflection remained a goal. The chapel garden was inspired by the intimate patio gardens of the Alhambra, and its gates were built on the pattern of the cloister gates at the Toledo Cathedral. Centered on a Spanish tiled fountain and encircled by cypresses, the garden's circular planting pattern, the "Gloriedas," symbolized the glory of God. Artwork also graced the chapel's 12,450-square-foot interior, which seats 600. A retinue of stained glass celebrates the Gospel and the liberal arts, while a hand carving of the Last Supper by the Italian sculptor Ernest Pelegrini stands above the altar.

Spanish tiles line the two loggias that connect the chapel and the Annie Russell, which is Florida's oldest and arguably most beautiful small theater. Funded by a gift from Mary Louise Curtis Bok Zimbalist (of the same family that built Bok Tower in Lake Wales), it was named for her close friend Annie Russell, an internationally acclaimed actress. The 377-seat theater was a modern interpretation of Italian Romanesque architecture (e.g., the Pisa Cathedral) constructed in the late Middle Ages. Arcaded loggias and galleries define the ground level, and a crenellated parapet surrounds the roof covering the stage area. The exterior's primary massing is a gabled main auditorium abutting a higher stage section, which has a tiered allotment of service rooms (fig. 7).[29]

Fig. 7. Kiehnel & Elliott's sketch of the Annie Russell Theatre, early 1930s.

Department of College Archives and Special Collections, Olin Library, Rollins College, Winter Park, Florida

Although the chapel and the theater were designed by different architects, the same contractor built them. The exterior walls of the buildings consist of terra-cotta tile and brick-surfaced textured stucco. Decorative details and trim are made of Florida travertine, while the roofs are covered in Spanish barrel tile. These features have remained consistent in Rollins's construction over the last century, as the campus has taken shape along the lines Hamilton Holt envisioned and now incorporates seventy-two buildings.

A NEW URBANISM REVIVAL

After spending a generation orienting the Rollins campus to the automobile, Holt's campus plan experienced a renaissance in the late 1990s, when the college and Winter Park partnered to champion a pedestrian-oriented urbanism. In 1997, the town-planning firm Dover-Kohl redesigned Park Avenue. Sidewalks were widened for outdoor dining, vehicular travel lanes were narrowed and bricked, and a prescription was provided to design buildings based on the principles of traditional civic art. The avenue took on a new life, and in 2002, Rollins College commissioned Chael Cooper & Associates, in affiliation with Dover-Kohl, to design the McKean Gateway and the Rinker admissions building at the entrance to the campus on Park Avenue (fig. 8). A decade later, ACI Architects designed the Rollins Gateway, which is modeled on the Harvard Gates and stands at the intersection of Fairbanks and Interlachen avenues (fig. 9). The Rollins Gateway also marks the terminus of a reconstructed axial walk centered on the Mills Building, which is now Rollins Hall, the epicenter of the college's liberal arts in action ethos that Holt championed.[30] Taken together, these projects document a return to the human-scaled architecture that was the hallmark of the American Renaissance.

"Stately Rollins College," a *New York Times* reporter notes, casts a definitive beauty in the theme world environs of Central Florida.[31] The college's aesthetic is grounded in Hamilton Holt's pragmatic vision of the liberal arts. Fred Rogers, the college's most noted alumnus, personifies this legacy. "Life is for Service," is carved in Florida travertine on the wall of a covered loggia, and Rogers carried a photograph of it in his wallet during his lifetime.[32] A timeless message, it invokes the Renaissance that began in Italy in the fifteenth century and continues to inspire more than a half millennium later.

Bruce Stephenson, is a planning consultant and a professor at Rollins College. His 2015 biography, *John Nolen, Landscape Architect and City Planner,* won the John Brinckerhoff Jackson Book Prize. He authored the concluding essay for *Iconic Planned Communities and the Challenge of Change* (2019), and his most recent book is *Stepping into Portland's Good Life: A Lesson in Sustainability* (2020).

Fig. 8. McKean Gateway and Marshall and Vera Lea Rinker Building by Chael, Cooper & Associates, 2002.

Fig. 9. Rollins Gateway by ACI Architects, 2012.

Notes

1. Henry Hope Reed, "Forward," in Geoffrey Scott, *The Architecture of Humanism* (New York: W.W. Norton: 1990), xiii.

2. Oliver Larkin, *Art and Life in America* (New York: Holt, Rinehart & Wilson, 1960), 293–300.

3. Edward Griggs, *The New Humanism* (New York: Huebsch, 1902), 212, 227.

4. Stanley Buder, *Visionaries and Planners: The Garden City Movement and the Modern Community* (New York: Oxford University Press, 1990), 72–73.

5. George Santayana, "The Intellectual Temper of the Age," *Winds of Doctrine* (New York: Charles Scribner, 1913), 1.

6. John Nolen, *Remodeling Roanoke* (Roanoke, VA: Stone Printing, 1907), 18.

7. Frederick Law Olmsted, "Preliminary Report upon the Proposed Suburb Village at Riverside," in *The Papers of Frederick Law Olmsted: Volume VI,* ed. David Schuyler and Jane Censer (Baltimore: Johns Hopkins University Press, 1992), 275.

8. Jack Lane, *Rollins College Centennial History: A Story of Perseverance, 1885–1985* (Orlando, FL: Story Farm, 2017).

9. Lewis Mumford, "The Intolerable City," *Harper's Monthly* (February 1926): 292.

10. Hamilton Holt, *Ideals for the Development of Rollins College* (June 1926), 1, Rollins College Archives and Special Collections (hereafter RA).

11. Hamilton Holt, letter to John Nolen, March 8, 1932, box 20, John Nolen Papers, Cornell University Manuscripts and Special Collections (hereafter NP).

12. John Nolen, letter to Hamilton Holt, March 3, 1932, box 20, NP.

13. John Nolen, "Common Places and Ideals of City Planning" (City Planning Exhibition, Jacksonville, Florida, October 29, 1925), box 74, NP.

14. John Nolen, "City Planning in Florida," *Suniland* (November 1925), 28, box 74, NP.

15. Vincent Scully, "The Architecture of Community," in *The New Urbanism: Toward an Architecture of Community*, ed. Peter Katz (New York: McGraw-Hill, 1994), 226.

16. R. Bruce Stephenson, *John Nolen: Landscape Architect and City Planner* (Amherst, MA; Massachusetts University Press, 2015), 192–200.

17. Ibid.

18. Arva Moore Parks, *George Merrick: Son of the South Wind: Visionary Creator of Coral Gables* (Gainesville, FL: University Press of Florida, 2015).

19. Holt, *Ideas for the Development of Rollins College,* 2–8.

20. "Description of the Building," Richard Kiehnel Folder, RA.

21. Robert Hughes, *American Visions: The Epic History of Art in America* (New York:

Alfred A. Knopf, 1997), 117–118.

22. Kenneth Clark, *Civilisation* (New York: Harpers & Row, 1969), 100.

23. Hamilton Holt, letter to Richard Kiehnel, August 16 and November 7, 1927, Richard Kiehnel Folder, RA.

24. Wenxian Zhang, *Rollins Architecture: A Pictorial Profile of Current and Historical Buildings*, 57, RA.

25. Ralph Cram, quoted in Jack Lane, "Knowles Memorial Chapel: Hamilton Holt's Gift to Rollins College," RA. https://blogs.rollins.edu/libraryarchives/2020/01/15/knowles-memorial-chapel-hamilton-holts-gift-to-rollins-college/

26. Zhang, *Rollins Architecture*, 81–82.

27. Ibid.

28. Lane, "Knowles Memorial Chapel."

29. National Register of Historic Places, "Annie Russell Theater," June 19, 1998.

30. The library was moved to the Olin Library in 1985.

31. Shaila Dewan, "36 Hours in Orlando," *New York Times*, April 6, 2011. https://www.nytimes.com/2011/03/06/travel/06hours-orlando.html

32. Darla Moore, "Life is for Service: The Words That Inspired Mr. Rogers," 2018. RA. http://blogs.rollins.edu/libraryarchives/2018/02/12/life-is-for-service-the-words-that-inspired-mister-rogers/

HENRY JOHN KLUTHO IN JACKSONVILLE

FROM CLASSICAL ARCHITECTURE TO THE PRAIRIE SCHOOL

WAYNE W. WOOD

On May 4, 1901, architect Henry John Klutho (1873–1964) was sitting at his desk in New York reading the newspaper. The main headline in the *New York Times* grabbed his attention: "Jacksonville, Fla. Swept by Flames … 130 Blocks of Residences and Business Houses Destroyed."

Jacksonville's Great Fire of May 3, 1901, was the largest conflagration to ever burn a city in the South. In the span of eight hours, in a single day, the fire—which had started a mattress-manufacturing plant on the far northwestern edge of town—had turned Jacksonville into a wasteland of ashes. Over 90 percent of downtown Jacksonville was incinerated, destroying 2,368 buildings, leveling 466 acres, and inflicting $15 million in property losses. Seeing an opportunity to rebuild an entire city from scratch and utilize his burgeoning architectural ideas, within two months, Klutho was living and working in Jacksonville.

THE YOUNG ARCHITECT

Klutho had grown up in the small town of Breese, Illinois. Even as a child, he demonstrated an artistic talent, and at age seventeen he enrolled in Schenk's Drawing Academy in St. Louis to further develop his graphic abilities. He then worked as apprentice with several St. Louis architects. After visiting the World's Columbian Exposition in Chicago in 1893, Klutho's commitment to become an architect was sealed. Although he was just twenty years old, the beauty of the elegant buildings at the fair spoke directly to his growing affection for classical architecture. The following year, he moved to New York City, where he apprenticed with a series of

Fig. 1. Thomas V. Porter residence, Jacksonville, Florida, 1902, by Henry John Klutho.

prominent architects, gaining valuable experience while immersing himself in traditional styles.

Eager to advance his skills, Klutho conferred with his father, who offered him two options. He would pay for his son to either go to the College of Architecture at MIT (one of the few architecture schools in existence at the time), or make an itinerary and arrangements to travel in Europe for a year, studying and sketching the great classical masterpieces in the tradition of Beaux-Arts training. Young Klutho chose the latter. After his European sojourn, he returned to New York in 1899 and opened his own architectural practice, where he remained for the next two years, until his move to Jacksonville, Florida.

RISING FROM JACKSONVILLE'S ASHES: AN INNOVATIVE CLASSICISM

Klutho quickly became a leader in Jacksonville's rebuilding effort. His fine artistic sense was matched by his sharp business acumen, and he impressed the town's movers and shakers with his abilities. The August 4, 1901 *Florida Times-Union & Citizen* newspaper announced that he had received the commission for the first building over three stories tall to be constructed since the Great Fire: "The design and plans for the handsome five-story business block to be erected by the Dyal-Upchurch Company, at a cost of $75,000.00, have been completed by architect H. J. Klutho, of New York City." Klutho described the style of the new building as "modern Renaissance."

In short order, he gained commissions for numerous civic, religious, and commercial buildings, as well as residences for wealthy citizens. His design for the new Jacksonville City Hall was a full expression of his Beaux-Arts training

Fig. 2. Jacksonville City Hall, 1902 (demolished 1960), by Henry John Klutho.

(fig. 2). Its first story was finished with Indiana limestone and granite-colored brick. The second story was faced with cream-colored brick capped by a copper cornice and balustrade. The dome and lantern were also copper-covered and featured an enormous four-faced Seth Thomas clock. The newspaper reported that the design was "in the style of the Modern French Renaissance––perhaps the most popular style with the prominent eastern Architects." The interior of Klutho's City Hall contained a grand marble staircase fourteen feet wide, surmounted on each side by clusters of incandescent globes. Over the staircase was a forty-foot-diameter dome, decorated with four lunette murals by New York artist John O'Neill. One of the mural sections was titled "Rebuilding" and allegorically represented the city recovering from the 1901 fire. The characters included an engineer, a mechanic, a laborer, and an architect holding the plans of the new city hall––obviously Klutho.

His most impressive residential commission was a classically inspired mansion for Thomas V. Porter, a governor of the Jacksonville Board of Trade. It featured a grand portico with two-story Corinthian columns, a mansard roof, and colonnaded porches on the sides of the house

Fig. 3. St. Clair-Abrams Mausoleum in Evergreen Cemetery, Jacksonville, 1901, by Henry John Klutho.

Fig. 4. Congregation Ahavath Chesed, Jacksonville, 1901, by Henry John Klutho.

(fig. 1). It cost $25,000, a substantial sum in 1902. Klutho described it as "Classic Colonial."

He had been in Jacksonville only three months when he received the smallest commission of his career, the St. Clair-Abrams Mausoleum in Evergreen Cemetery (fig. 3). This elegant tomb embodied the grace and symmetry of a Greek shrine. It was constructed of white Georgia marble, with a copper cornice and cross, as well as a well-designed wrought-iron gate. He also received commissions for numerous churches, including First Baptist Church, one of the city's best Romanesque designs, and a synagogue for Congregation Ahavath Chesed, which had a traditional classical facade (fig. 4).

In 1903, Klutho won the competition to design the new public library, to be built with funds donated by philanthropist Andrew Carnegie. The result was a splendid Renaissance temple, one of the most perfect classical compositions of his career (fig. 5). Here, Klutho showed his inclination toward innovation in the generous use of copper for the entablature and pediment and the inclusion of the heads of great men of art and science within the Ionic capitals of the portico. The faces of Aristotle, Euclid, Shakespeare, Herodotus, and Plato gazed down on all who entered—a fitting entryway for a place of learning. The copper embellishments and the figural transformations of column capitals would reappear in Klutho's subsequent designs. The facade was constructed of smooth-cut limestone, and its interior featured an art-glass skylight.

His reputation as a master of the classical vocabulary spread to nearby cities. In Savannah, Georgia, he won two commissions for office buildings, the National Bank of Savannah and the Germania Bank and Office Building. Both designs were in Klutho's modern

Fig. 5. Carnegie Library (Jacksonville Public Library), Jacksonville, opened 1905, by Henry John Klutho.

Renaissance style. Neither building was ever constructed. He also entered a design competition for Savannah's City Hall. His robust Beaux-Arts plan featured many of the classical trappings of his Jacksonville City Hall, including a dome, but his design was not chosen.

One of Klutho's most prestigious commissions was the new Governor's Mansion in Tallahassee, which featured a colonnade of massive Ionic columns, wrapping around three sides and paired at the extruded porticos—aggrandizing otherwise modest dimensions (see page 40, fig. 2). Klutho was also one of two finalists in a design competition to create a campus for the new University of Florida in Gainesville. His master plan, a tapestry of stately classical buildings, was sensitively designed to harmonize with the rolling land covered with oak and pine forests. Only his drawings for the library, administration building, and one classroom building have survived. Ultimately, the university selected William Augustus Edwards, who designed its early buildings in the Gothic Revival style, prevalent in campus construction at the time.

Klutho was successful in obtaining two other commissions outside Jacksonville. Stetson University in DeLand, Florida, chose him to design its Carnegie Library. Its traditional Beaux-Arts facade is highlighted by a portico colonnade of the Ionic order, and in the pediment is an abstract geometric composition of a circle flanked by two triangles. The roof fascia is accentuated with classical dentils, below which Klutho placed the names of authors––Tennyson, Longfellow, Chaucer, Shakespeare, Browning, and Lanier––as well as an inscription, "Knowledge is Power." Another fine Beaux-Arts design was the Marion County Courthouse in Ocala, Florida. It was constructed of local limestone and featured a massive entrance flanked

Fig. 6. Klutho residence on Main Street, Jacksonville, by Henry John Klutho, 1908.

by Doric columns and small domes surmounting very large pilasters. A central octagonal cupola was capped by a dome containing four large clocks.

Klutho was a man of the latest fashion—not just in architecture but in social thinking, automobiles, and clothing. His eye for beauty was unerring, and when he met the very beautiful Elizabeth Wicker, it was the beginning of a period of great change in his life.

THE WRIGHT MOMENT

Klutho and Elizabeth Wicker were married in June 1904, and the following month they went on their honeymoon to Niagara Falls. While there, Klutho heard of an outspoken architect who was building two prominent new buildings in nearby Buffalo. Before returning from his honeymoon, Klutho went by to visit this architect: Frank Lloyd Wright. Wright gave him a tour of both buildings under construction—the Darwin Martin residence, one of his finest "Prairie"-style houses, and the Larkin Administration Building, a revolutionary high-rise that would transform business work spaces in America.

He also showed him the Prudential Building, an early skyscraper designed by Louis Sullivan, whom Wright considered to be his mentor. Sullivan, Wright, and their followers were part of a movement that sought to establish a new style of architecture eschewing European influence and indigenous to America, calling for a close relationship between a building and its environment. With its flowing spaces, natural materials, and broad expanses of windows, this new movement—later called the "Prairie School"—found its maestro in Louis Sullivan, but Frank Lloyd Wright was its most talented and prolific proponent. Klutho was enormously impressed with Wright and came home to Jacksonville inspired by what he had seen and heard; yet he was challenged by the conflict between these ideas and his traditional architectural training.

In the years that followed, Klutho gradually began to forge his own path. Each new commission presented the opportunity to explore the new direction. In early 1907, he was selected to design Jacksonville's new YMCA, and his original plans showed a typical classical facade with Doric columns and rusticated arches. Several months into the project, he abruptly revised the plans to eliminate all traces of its classical elements. He contracted with the Southern Ferro Concrete Company of Atlanta to build the first reinforced-concrete building in the South, featuring large plate-glass windows and clean lines that expressed the internal structure of the building. Klutho's description of the YMCA was significant in revealing his new direction:

The new building represents a style of architecture which is neither classic nor Renaissance, but in line with a new style being evolved in this country typifying the American character, i.e., strong and massive in its general outline, large moldings, and void of useless ornamentation; square openings, horizontal lines and straightforward in general design. The whole building is conspicuous for its simplicity and dignity.

The YMCA building was Klutho's first and somewhat tentative step toward embracing the Chicago movement. His next project went even further. For developer William A. Bisbee, he created a ten-story, reinforced-concrete-frame high-rise—Florida's first true skyscraper. Its facade was faced with polished limestone and abstract, geometric terra-cotta ornaments. It featured broad plate-glass "Chicago-style" windows. The tall, thin tower soared above Jacksonville's three- and four-story skyline and was the talk of the town. The excitement created by the Bisbee Building resulted in its being entirely rented before its completion, so Mr. Bisbee ordered Klutho to "double it," resulting in the final building being constructed two bays wide.

Klutho's full commitment to the Prairie School was exhibited in the home he designed for his own family, a consummately Prairie-style house, with broad, six-foot overhangs projecting over continuous bands of windows. Leaded glass with the "Tree of Life" design stepped up the north side of the house, defining the stairway as well as lighting it. Local residents were astonished by this radical house situated prominently on Main Street (fig. 6).

BUILDING A NEW CITY

Soon, another Prairie-style masterpiece followed: the Seminole Hotel. It was originally slated to be a bank and office building, but the initial owner, the Utica Investment Company, went bankrupt just as the steel frame of the building topped out at ten stories. The new owner ordered Klutho to change it from an office building to a hotel, which altered the room sizes, the plumbing, and other features. The task was all the more daunting due to the owner's insistence that the building open as scheduled, on January 1, 1910. The external decoration of the structure had already been set, with a row of Native American heads at the second-story level. Although these heads were originally destined to represent the Utica tribe from upstate New York, the name of the building was revised as so that they could now represent Florida's native Seminole people. The facade of the Seminole Hotel was Klutho's first commercial statement in the Prairie School idiom. The vertical brick pilasters with abstract capitals made of cross motifs were highly reminiscent of those on Frank Lloyd Wright's Larkin Building.

After the Seminole Hotel, in a commission from the Jacksonville Shriners, Klutho incorporated Prairie School principles into the Masonic requirements for a building based on ancient designs. The exotic fusion of an Egyptian Revival-style temple with the bold geometry of the Prairie School garnered national notoriety. The building's plan is indebted to Frank Lloyd Wright's Unity Temple in Oak Park, Illinois, and its rich terra-cotta ornamentation paid homage to that of Louis Sullivan. The Morocco Temple was crowned by a series of horizontal metal cornices, which served as a culmination for the facade's abstract capitals and gave balance to the composition. Sadly, these were removed in the 1950s, and currently preservationists are urging that they be restored.

Klutho, who was of German ancestry, was active in the Germania Club, a social organization for Jacksonville's large German community, for which he designed a new clubhouse in 1912. This riverfront building became a highly visible landmark, with a magnificent circular portal facing the street. The arch contained a geometric grille of metal and glass twenty-five feet in diameter, making it one of Klutho's more eclectic Prairie-style designs.

The most challenging job in Klutho's career was the four-story St. James Building, for the Cohen Brothers' Department Store, which covered an entire city block (fig. 7). It was an innovative, mixed-use concept in which small, privately run shops were located on the ground-floor periphery; a massive department store filled the center of the first story and all of the second story; and two floors of professional office space were located above the store. When it opened in 1912, it was the largest building in Jacksonville and the ninth-largest department store in the United States.

The St. James was richly decorated with terra-cotta Sullivanesque ornamentation, abstractly depicting spiral seashell motifs and likenesses of plants native to Florida.

Fig. 7. St. James Building, Jacksonville, opened 1912 as the Cohen Brothers Department Store, by Henry John Klutho.

Fig. 8. Florida Life Insurance Building, 1912, by Henry John Klutho. Photographed in 1987, before the removal of its terra-cotta capitals.

Its interior was a tour de force: a huge octagonal glass dome, seventy-five feet in diameter and supported by eight colossal heroic statues, flooded the two-story department store with sunlight. In 1997, Klutho's magnum opus was renovated to become Jacksonville's present-day City Hall.

Simultaneously with the St. James, Klutho was designing the Florida Life Insurance Building, which would be recognized as one of the great Prairie School skyscrapers in all America. It was a narrow, beautifully proportioned tower that soared vertically, giving an impression of being much taller than its eleven-story height. The lower two stories formed the tower's base, abundantly adorned with glazed terra-cotta. Broad plate-glass Chicago-style windows accentuated the facade, drawing the eye upward along the slender pilasters to a crowning burst of terra-cotta scrollwork that supported an ornate copper cornice. Klutho's skyscraper was actually the embodiment of a classical column, translated into the new vernacular of the Prairie School. Its distinct base,

shaft, and capital are a symbolic tribute to the pillars of his classical architectural training (fig. 8).

Plans are currently underway to return this building to its former glory, including the restoration of the beautiful terra-cotta stylized capitals that were removed in 1994.

The lost commission that haunted Klutho the most was also a harbinger of changes in his architectural style. In 1916, New York architect Kenneth Murchison won a design competition for the new Jacksonville railway terminal. Klutho had submitted an imposing Prairie-style design that would have been one of the most notable of his career. However, Murchison's winning design was a massive neoclassical temple that freely plagiarized the facade of New York's Pennsylvania Station. It featured a colonnade of colossal Doric columns, each forty-two feet tall. The monumental design readily appealed to the sense of power and gravitas that the railroad moguls wished to convey, and Klutho's more esoteric design lost out.

Fig. 9: Larimer Memorial Library (now Larimer Arts Center), Palatka, Florida, 1929, by Henry John Klutho.

THE LATER YEARS

By the close of World War I, the Prairie style was waning in popularity. Magazines such as *Ladies' Home Journal*, which had once heavily promoted the new architectural vogue, now moved on to more popular postwar trends. Throughout Florida, the real estate boom of the 1920s was taking root, and the new communities that were sprouting up across the state had Spanish and Italian themes, retrospectively called "Mediterranean Revival."

Klutho, whose German heritage led to a diminishment of his reputation after the United States entered World War I, never regained the success he had enjoyed in the heyday of his Prairie School era. He returned to his classical roots in creating a major addition to the Florida State Capitol Building in 1921, and he also designed several exemplary Mediterranean-style residences in the 1920s. One of his final noteworthy buildings was a small library in Palatka, Florida. The Larimer Memorial Library, designed in 1929, combined both classical and Prairie-style themes, a fitting coda to his life's body of work (fig. 9). Klutho died in 1964, the latter part of his career having coincided with the Great Depression and World War II. Nonetheless, his legacy lives on in his unique collection of grand classical and Prairie School buildings, a Florida architectural treasure.

Wayne W. Wood, O.D., Hon. A.I.A, is Historian-at-Large for the Jacksonville (Florida) Historical Society and has written numerous books on Northeast Florida history and architecture. He is the founder of Riverside Avondale Preservation, one of the largest neighborhood preservation groups in the South. He has lectured extensively and written numerous articles about Henry John Klutho. He lives one of the premier Prairie-style houses in Florida.

References

Broward, Robert C. *The Architecture of Henry John Klutho: The Prairie School in Jacksonville.* Jacksonville, FL: Jacksonville Historical Society, 2003.

———. *A Prairie School Masterpiece: The History of the St. James Building.* Jacksonville,

FL: Jacksonville Historical Society, 1997.

The Western Architect. Vol. 20, no. 6. Minneapolis, MN: June 1914.

Wood, Wayne W. *The Great Fire of 1901.* Jacksonville, FL: Jacksonville Historical Society, 2001.

———. *Jacksonville's Architectural Heritage: Landmarks for the Future.* Jacksonville, FL: Jacksonville Historic Landmarks Commission, University of North Florida Press, 1989.

DISCOVERING ADDISON MIZNER

THE ELUSIVE LEGACY OF PALM BEACH'S MOST IMPORTANT ARCHITECT

BETH DUNLOP

For more than a century, the architect Addison Mizner (1872–1933) has been both adulated and excoriated. He had an enormous and fertile capacity for both invention and appropriation, and over the years he was regarded as a genius or a charlatan—or sometimes both. He had a generosity of wit, an ability to develop strong friendships, and a much-celebrated presence. He was revered as a genius, and yet at times he was ridiculed for overselling his dreams and fantasies and overspending his clients' money. His mixed reputation derives from his rather indelible personality as well as his body of work. But it also stems from both the changing architectural trends and the rapidly changing world of the early and middle twentieth century. Fame was to become as much a burden as a blessing. With his writer-pundit brother, Wilson Mizner, he enjoyed a national reputation, enough so that the completion of a house or building in Palm Beach was often reported in newspapers across the country. Some, or all, of those sometimes contradictory descriptions are true, and they have lived on through the mythmaking that surrounds places such as Palm Beach.

Widely traveled, Addison Mizner had spent his early years as a gold prospector, an importer of fruit and coffee, a commercial artist, and more. And though he apprenticed with Willis Polk from 1893 to 1896 in San Francisco, he did not begin to practice architecture until much later when he lived in New York. During his time in New York, starting in 1904, he attained wide social popularity, ensuring his own status and the clients who were to come, but little architectural acclaim, though he did design three houses that were in what was termed the Spanish style.[1]

Fig. 1. Everglades Club on Worth Avenue, opened 1919, Addison Mizner's first commission in Palm Beach, Florida.

It was not until he moved to Palm Beach in 1918, however, that he gained full notice as an architect—or for that matter, built up a body of work. By the 1920s, Palm Beach had become the seasonal home to members of a new American aristocracy that emerged from the Industrial Revolution with fortunes in steel, coal, transportation, shipping, finance, dry goods, and even Jell-O—and their lives were well documented in the newspapers of the day, including the elaborate and extravagant winter houses they built in Palm Beach and the architect who designed them. Mizner was lured to Palm Beach by his friend Paris Singer, an heir to the eponymous sewing machine fortune, to design what was originally intended to be a convalescent home for World War I veterans. Begun in 1918, the project soon morphed into something far different, an exclusive private club, Today, more than a century later, the Everglades Club (fig. 1) remains a symbol of status, wealth, and exclusivity, but it is also still a showcase of Mizner's work—and one that seems to be able to impart many of the architect's ideas to a larger public, without opening its doors to them.

An un-bylined column in the *Palm Beach Post* offered this anticipatory appreciation of what would become Mizner's hallmark architecture: "Instead of repeating the common and hideous mistake that has been perpetrated all through Florida of using a style of architecture adapted to northern surroundings and bleak and repellant climate, he has searched Italy, Spain and Northern Africa for a model, and has used a blended, softened type of color and line that will prove a revelation." The writer went on to depict Mizner's more narrative approach to architecture as an example of the "feudal, medieval, Italian, Spanish style" and described the building as an evolved medieval castle that had evolved first, perhaps, into a monastery and then more, its imaginary moat filled up over the centuries.[2]

Fig. 2. Louwana, an early Palm Beach residential commission (for Gurnee Munn and his wife, Marie Louise Wanamaker Munn, whose family started the Wanamaker department store in Philadelphia), by Addison Mizner, 1919.

As the Everglades Club came to fruition, Mizner began designing houses that were at once grand and evocative. He filled these houses with European plunder (as was typical of the times), ranging from single pieces of furniture to entire ceilings, but could not buy enough to support the demand in Palm Beach and thus established Mizner Industries to provide himself with stone, tile, iron, furniture, and decorative objects. El Mirasol, designed for the Edward Stotesburys (and tragically demolished in 1959), was built in 1919 and quickly followed by Casa Amado (for Charles Munn), Louwana (for Gurnee Munn), and El Solano (figs. 2, 4), which Mizner designed for himself but almost immediately sold to Harold S. Vanderbilt. The subsequent six years were prolific ones for Mizner, but by 1925, he had turned his sights to a larger scheme, that of creating a new resort town in Boca Raton. By then, he had been part of several such land development dreams; two years before, he

was a central figure in the plan to turn a swath of beach-front land into a sporting resort featuring golf and polo, anchored by the Gulf Stream Golf Club, which Mizner designed. By the time was concentrating on Boca, the Florida land boom was growing wobbly, and although he completed the centerpiece hotel, the Cloister Inn (fig. 3), and several administration buildings, Mizner found himself in bankruptcy and returned to Palm Beach where he continued his architectural practice, though at a much slower pace, until he died in 1933.

The booming 1920s turned to the 1930s and '40s, and as modernism took hold, Mizner's star fell.[3] His reputation was further assailed by the publication, first in *The New Yorker* magazine and then as a book published in 1953, of an excoriating look at both Wilson and Addison Mizner written by Alva Johnston.[4] Though Johnston's primary victim (and that is not too harsh a word) was Wilson

Mizner, he did not spare Addison, coining the phrase "Bastard-Spanish-Moorish-Romanesque-Gothic-Renaissance-Bull-Market-Damn-the-Expense." Johnston's book, later to become the source material for a failed Stephen Sondheim musical,[5] also perpetuated many myths about Mizner as an architect, painting him as a forgetful dilettante—a subject of sensationalist journalism and speculation. In some ways, he was a victim of his own self-deprecating wit, but he was also subject to long-running rumors, such as the often repeated (and false) assertion that he occasionally forgot to include stairways in the drawings for some of his more lavish houses.

Redemption came slowly, in the form of two works of scholarship, the first by the curator and museum director Christina Orr-Cahall, who wrote about Mizner in her unpublished doctoral dissertation for Yale University. Subsequently, in 1977, as chief curator (and then director) of the Norton Gallery, now the Norton Museum of Art, she mounted a multi-venue exhibition devoted to Mizner's Palm Beach work, complete with a catalogue, both entitled *Addison Mizner: Architect of Dreams and Realities*.[6] And in 1984, the historian Donald Curl, a professor of history at Florida Atlantic University, wrote a fine and well-researched biography[7] of Mizner that laid the groundwork for much of the scholarship to follow, including my own.[8] In recent years, access to more source materials, including Mizner's scrapbooks,[9] has offered new insight into the depth of his knowledge and breadth of his source material.[10] Just as helpful is the newly searchable digitization of 16,800 newspapers (and thus millions of newspaper editions) from across the United States and around the world dating back to the eighteenth century.[11]

What emerges from all this, in an unclouded look at the accounts of his life and work, is that, too often, the force of his personality and the fame of his clients have obscured the clearer window through which both Mizner and his architecture should be viewed—one that acknowledges the breadth and depth of his knowledge of architectural history and the decorative arts, his innate understanding of both proportion and perspective, and his ability to meld both classicism and urbanism in his projects. In the course of the fifteen or so years Mizner worked in Palm Beach, he designed approximately one hundred private houses, most of which were in Palm Beach or Boca Raton (most of the latter were smaller houses that were

Fig. 3. Passageway at the Cloister Inn (now part of the Boca Raton Resort and Club), Boca Raton, Florida, by Addison Mizner, 1926, photographed c. 1928.

intended for less affluent buyers in Mizner's idealized city there). Of these, including the twenty-nine houses in Boca's Old Floresta neighborhood, more than seventy were built. A handful of these were in other locations: in Pebble Beach, for his niece; Montecito, California; Bryn Mawr, Pennsylvania; Colorado Springs, Colorado; and St. Petersburg, Florida. He also designed civic and institutional structures, including private clubs and churches (among them, the Gulf Stream Golf Club [fig. 5] and Boynton Woman's Club near Palm Beach; the Cloister in Sea Island, Georgia; and Riverside Baptist Church in Jacksonville, Florida), established a decorative arts manufactory to fill his buildings, and more.[12]

The work in Palm Beach and beyond was a pastiche that drew from Spain, Italy, France, Morocco, Mexico, and Central America, and more antiquarian inspirations such as Roman or Byzantine architecture. It set the standard for much that was to follow, in terms of both aesthetics and an approach to craft, as many of Mizner's carpenters and artisans went on to find work elsewhere in Florida. Applying the techniques they had learned in Palm Beach, they spread this new approach to architecture—part pictorial and part collage—establishing the essentially fictitious Mediterranean style as emblematic of boom-time Florida. He drew not just from his early experiences as a child in Northern California and Central

Fig. 4. El Solano, which Addison Mizner initially built for himself in Palm Beach in 1925 before selling it to Harold S. Vanderbilt.

Fig. 5. Gulf Stream Golf Club, Gulf Stream, Florida, by Addison Mizner, 1924.

Fig. 6. Villa Flora, Palm Beach, by Addison Mizner, 1923.

America and his subsequent travels but also from his encyclopedic knowledge of historic architecture and decorative arts and his equally encyclopedic storybook imagination. In Palm Beach, as the new moneyed class asserted its new and sometimes fabricated pedigree, Mizner was able, in architecture, to create a sense of pedigree in houses that imparted an almost entirely invented lineage.

In 1923, Cooper C. Lightbown, then mayor of Palm Beach, observed: "The style of architecture which is being developed in Palm Beach is unique. It certainly is not Spanish—it comes nearer being Italian. But the combination of ideas, worked out by the school of architects of which Addison

Fig. 7. Lagomar, Palm Beach, featuring a Spanish octagonal ceiling, terra-cotta tiled floors, and wrought–iron details, by Addison Mizner, 1924.

Mizner is the preeminent exponent, is typically Palm Beach. I believe the day is coming when it will be referred to as the Mizner school of architecture and students will come here from all parts of the world to study it, just as now they go to Europe."[13]

Though the mayor's prophesy did not materialize, there is a renewed interest in Mizner's level of scholarship, thanks to the newly available sources. As much as anything, the scrapbooks underscore his voracious appetite for history, information, and imagery—all of which play such a fundamental role is his work.

While there is no written evidence to back this up, a more general understanding of

Fig. 8. La Guerida, designed for department store magnate Rodman Wanamaker by Addison Mizner in 1923 and subsequently occupied by six generations of Joseph P. Kennedy Sr.'s family.

Fig. 9. Via Mizner, Worth Avenue, Palm Beach, 1923. The arcaded pedestrian "village" features shops, offices, and residences, including the five-story Villa Mizner, which was designed and inhabited by the architect.

that very particular time period after World War I suggests that Mizner was reflecting some of the most advanced cultural and critical thinking of the times. Steeped in the classical vocabulary of his predecessors, his work also adopted the methods of collage and montage that were being explored in early modern painting and film, the latter most significantly in the work and writing of Sergei Eisenstein in Russia. The advent of the movies, too, gave more credence to the idea that one could recreate entire other worlds, and that they need not be as much authentic as evocative.[14]

Mizner designed and built a group of extraordinarily beautiful houses, yet his legacy is not so much in individual buildings as in laying groundwork for a new world of community building throughout Florida. Connecting the traditions of the Mediterranean and

Fig. 10. Villa Mizner, detail.

the Caribbean with stage-set fantasies that offered an escape to a new life would prove to encourage a similar approach—looking both backward and forward—in the Florida architecture that followed: Art Deco, the theatrical inventions of Morris Lapidus, Disney World, and even, it can be said, New Urbanism.

Beth Dunlop, is a writer and editor specializing in architecture, interior design, and landscape. Her newest (and twenty-ninth) book is *Addison Mizner: Architect of Fantasy and Romance*. Among her other books are *Miami: Mediterranean Splendor and Deco Dreams* and *The Tropical Cottage: At Home in Coconut Grove*. With Joanna Lombard, she coauthored *Great Houses of Florida* and *DPZ: The Architecture of Duany and Plater-Zyberk*. A 2018 Alicia Patterson Fellow, Dunlop was a Pulitzer Prize-nominated architecture critic for the *Miami Herald*. She was editor of *Modern Magazine* and, before that, *HOME Miami* magazine. An alumna of Vassar College, she lives in Miami Beach, Florida.

Notes

1. Donald W. Curl, *Mizner's Florida: American Resort Architecture* (Cambridge, MA: MIT Press, 1984), 16–37.

2. *Palm Beach Post*, October 27, 1918.

3. Though, in fact, Palm Beach has few modernist buildings. Alternatively, the midcentury Palm Beach taste leaned toward architect John Volk's personalized version of Bahamian/Caribbean architecture as well as a version of the Hollywood Regency style—modern but not really modernist.

4. Alva Johnston, *The Legendary Mizners* (New York: Farrar, Straus & Young, 1953). (A note in the not always reliable Wikipedia points out that this work has been "superseded" by subsequent biographies.)

5. *Road Show* by Stephen Sondheim and John Weidman, 1999.

6. Christina Orr-Cahall, *Addison Mizner: Architect of Dreams and Realities* (West Palm Beach, FL: Norton Gallery of Art), 1977.

7. Curl, *Mizner's Florida*.

8. Other subsequent biographical publications include Caroline Seebohm, *Boca Rococo: How Addison Mizner Invented Florida's Gold Coast* (New York: Clarkson Potter, 2001); and Stephen Perkins and James Caughman, *Addison Mizner: The Architect Whose Genius Defined Palm Beach* (Guilford, CT: Lyons Press, 2018). In my 2019 book, *Addison Mizner: Architect of Fantasy and Romance* (Rizzoli), I took a somewhat different tack from the preceding volumes on Mizner.

9. These are in the possession of the Society of the Four Arts in Palm Beach, where a large number of them have been scanned and digitized and are in the public domain.

10. The notebooks, part of the Mizner Library at the Society of the Four Arts in Palm Beach, were not publicly accessible before digitization, due to their fragility.

11. www.newspapers.com.

12. These numbers are gleaned in part from records, as well as from both Orr-Cahall, *Addison Mizner: Architect of Dreams and Realities*, and Curl, *Mizner's Florida*. To my knowledge, there is no definitive accounting of Mizner's built and unbuilt works.

13. "Castles in Spain are Drab Huts Beside Palm Beach, Lightbown Says," *Palm Beach Post,* May 26, 1923.

14. Mizner was known as a frequent patron of the movies, reportedly taking up four seats because of his girth.

CLASSICAL FLORIDA
A BRIEF HISTORY

ELIZABETH PLATER-ZYBERK

"The Mediterranean, Caribbean and Gulf of Mexico form a homogeneous, though interrupted, sea."—A. J. Liebling

Florida was conceived underwater, its geology a limestone structure of porous coral rock created by sea creatures. Destined again to submerge as seas rise, it faces the prospect, some say, of an Anthropocene Atlantis. The peninsula has long been a place of coming and going, both of land and people: the land, often elevated to enable farming and building, or dug out to make more water; the people, seeking a new life in migration, annually or permanently.

The first human residents of Florida were Native Americans. Various tribes cultivated the land and built sheltering mounds and light structures of palm trunks and fronds.[1] The Miccosukee are their surviving presence, continuing tribal traditions in and near the Everglades.

The arrival of Europeans, Caribbeans, and Africans in the sixteenth century brought settlement and building that reflected the provenance of the diaspora. The newcomers were attracted to miraculous promise, starting with Ponce de Léon's mythical Fountain of Youth, and continuing to this day in Florida's annual reception of a city's worth of new residents.

BEGINNINGS

The earliest permanent buildings were the stone and stucco structures of St. Augustine (founded in 1565)—courtyard buildings, a type prevalent throughout the Mediterranean and Spanish-settled Central and South America. The British succession in the eighteenth century introduced wood building techniques. The

Fig. 1. Freedom Tower (formerly Miami Daily News and Metropolis Building), Miami, by Schultze & Weaver, completed 1925.

clapboard second stories added to the Spaniards' first floors in St. Augustine proved to be a logical climatic response. Durable masonry meeting the ground, with wood frame and light sheathing above, seeking the breezes, became a style repeated throughout the Caribbean. In Key West, nineteenth-century shipbuilders applied their skills to tongue-and-groove interiors and Victorian embellishments. As the state's reputation as a holiday destination flourished, this construction tradition was applied to the large porched hotels of Palm Beach, Belleair, Miami, and Boca Grande, where the Gasparilla Inn—the only remaining example of these—displays a tall, classical front porch.[2]

By the late nineteenth century, northern Florida could be considered part of the developing world of the United States. St. Augustine had evolved as a winter resort, and Jacksonville pursued big-city aspirations after a devastating fire in 1901 destroyed much of the town. In Tallahassee, the preparation for Florida's statehood in 1845 had produced a capitol building mirroring the classicism of its siblings across the country, as did the first Governor's Mansion (fig. 2) somewhat later. Orlando and its environs, including Winter Park, turned to a Mediterranean vernacular.[3]

Meanwhile, other parts of the state were still barely accessible, hostile to overland travel and abundant in swamps and mosquitos. Travelers by sea from the north aimed for Key West, where settlement was already a century advanced, and where shoal-draft boats could be hired for coastal destinations to the north. Henry Flagler's extension of the railroad to Palm Beach in 1894, to Miami in 1896, and to Key West in 1912 opened South Florida to a belated colonization.

THE TWENTIETH CENTURY

Three architectures inaugurated twentieth-century South Florida. Lightweight wood-frame structures raised above crawl spaces, shedding thermal load, and with porches offering protection from the sun, displayed their African provenance. These evolved into the Mission-style bungalows built by arrivals from New England and New York's Adirondacks. By the 1920s, masonry was deemed a hardier response to humidity, insects, and hurricanes. To this day, subtropical Florida is the only part of the United States where virtually all building consists of bearing-wall masonry. Masonry construction also enabled the conceptual connection to a longer history of Western culture—with sources from Greece, Rome, and indeed the entire Mediterranean—to give stature to the new world. In this, Florida joined the national trend of the City Beautiful movement and, later, the civic building of the WPA. With the advent of the International Style, classically trained architects applied the fashions of Art Deco and Moderne to buildings of the 1930s and '40s, especially in Miami Beach. In the boom years following World War II, these origins were largely set aside, replaced by other masonry modernisms, the kitsch of Morris Lapidus, and Brazilian modernism. Nevertheless, these three forms still can be seen across the state as a visible chronology of the growing new cities.

Fig. 2. Original Florida Governor's Mansion, Tallahassee (demolished), by Henry John Klutho, completed 1907.

Classical architecture as promoted by the Ecole de Beaux-Arts in the nineteenth century was the foundation for all three traditions. At the time of these earliest Florida buildings, the new world's architects were seasoned travelers, visiting European sites.[4] Large-format photographic folios recorded their observations of the monuments of old-world cities and of the vernacular structures of the European countryside. Almost exact replicas of European precedents can be found across Florida, including in the Villages of Coral Gables. Travelers within the hemisphere absorbed the Central American and Caribbean interpretations of European roots. Addison Mizner's sketchbooks of his trips to Central America, for example, informed his work in Palm Beach and Boca Raton, in turn a powerful influence on other architects.[5]

Mizner's contemporaries in Palm Beach included Maurice Fatio, Josef Urban, John Volk, Henry S. Harvey and L. Philips Clarke (Palm Beach Town Hall), Gustav Adam Maass, Marion Sims Wyeth (who as late as 1955 produced a new Classical Revival Governor's Mansion in Tallahassee), and others. The earlier deployment of Classical Revival in Palm Beach (Whitehall, Flagler's mansion of 1902; fig. 3) gave way to Mediterranean compositions. Examples include Paul Chalfin and Francis Burrall Hoffman's Vizcaya (1922, for James Deering; fig. 4) in Miami, and L. Dwight Baum's Cà d'Zan (1924, for the Ringling family; see p. 57) in Sarasota, made of building elements and furnishings sold by Europeans after World War I, and extensive formal gardens. The gardens of Florida follow the national trajectory of traditional formal and picturesque compositions, applied with subtropical horticulture.

The hotels of this era evolved from the modest wood structures that first welcomed wintering northerners to elaborate scene-sets, often referring to Renaissance monuments, seeking with fantasy and glamour to obliterate memory of war and influenza. The Schultze & Weaver design for The Breakers hotel in Palm Beach (see p. 54) was modeled on the Villa Medici in Rome. The Giralda tower of Seville was inspiration, as it had been for McKim, Mead & White's Madison Square Garden, for three Schultze & Weaver towers in Miami: the Roney Plaza, no longer standing; the Miami News

Fig. 3. Whitehall, Palm Beach, by Carrère & Hastings, completed 1902. The former winter residence of industrialist Henry Flagler, it is now the Henry Morrison Flagler Museum.

Fig. 4. Villa Vizcaya, Miami, by F. Burrall Hoffman (Paul Chalfin, design director, and Diego Suarez, landscape designer), 1914–22.

Tower (now known as Freedom Tower for its role in the arrival of the Cuban diaspora of the 1960s, fig. 1); and the Biltmore hotel (see p. 52), still an astonishing focal presence in Coral Gables. Schultze & Weaver also expanded Mizner's Cloister Inn in Boca Raton.

These resort developments laid the foundation for permanent communities, a successional urban development protocol still widespread in our time. For Coral Gables, George Merrick's grand vision of a Mediterranean city, a cadre of architects was imported from the north to design tens of buildings in short order. Among these were Walter deGarmo, Denman and George Fink, Martin Luther Hampton, Phineas Paist, Harold Steward, John and Coulton Skinner, and Henry Killam Murphy. The 1928 City Hall (fig. 5), by Paist and Denman Fink, was a direct reference to William Strickland's Greek Revival Philadelphia Bourse of 1834. Two dozen "villages" of exotic styles were intended to seed development across the city. Seven of the Coral Gables Villages were completed and still enchant: French City, French Country, French Normandy, Florida Pioneer, Italian, Chinese, and Dutch South African (see p. 53). Philip Goodwin, who partnered with Edward Durell Stone on the Museum of Modern Art in New York, designed French Country houses, and Mott B. Schmidt created superb French City houses. Marion

Sims Wyeth designed the Dutch South African Village and, with the same floor plans, a Persian Village that was not built.[6]

The civic buildings represented the belief in a long-term future. In downtown Miami, Paist & Steward's federal courthouse (see p. 48) was made entirely of local limestone, with elaborate moldings textured by the coral shell deposits. The nearby Central Baptist Church (Dougherty & Gardner, 1926) faced intersecting streets, each with an arched Ionic portico. The traditional distinction between urban fabric and civic buildings was clear: the houses of Coral Gables were picturesque compositions in a Mediterranean style, while the civic buildings followed a classical mode.

The entire state rewards the search for early classical treasures. Among them are St. Petersburg's Open Air Post Office (George Stuart, 1917, see p. 56), Sarasota County Courthouse (Dwight James Baum, 1927, see p. 57), the Sarasota Post Office (George Albree Freeman, 1931), the Tampa Federal Courthouse, now a hotel (James Knox Taylor, 1905), and other buildings, including railway stations and churches. Such a tour of early beauties should not neglect the 1920s movie theaters, with "atmospheric" interiors giving the illusion of being outdoors in a Spanish or Italian courtyard, including

Fig. 5. City Hall, Coral Gables, by Phineas Paist and Harold Steward (Denman Fink, artistic advisor), completed 1928,

two by John Eberson in 1926—the Tampa Theater and, in Miami, the Olympia Theater.

There is still much to be done in the way of documentation and examination of this early architecture. But informal observations can be made. For instance, in a comparison of contemporary phases of the architecture of Florida and California, in the references to Spain, one might observe very different compositional strategies. This can be seen in their iconic representatives, the Santa Barbara County Courthouse (William Mooser, 1929) and the Coral Gables Douglas Entrance (DeGarmo, Paist, and Fink, 1924, see p. 51). The California tradition, influenced by the Spanish missions, evolved into a scenographic approach to facade composition—architectural elements picturesquely arranged on a single plane. In contrast, Florida's three-dimensional massing of adjacent elements, each symmetrical and able to stand alone, emerged under the influence of Central America and Cuba, with their already well-established tradition of neoclassical composition. The Central American ornamental influence is exemplified in Kiehnel & Elliott's Coral Gables Congregational Church of 1923 (see p. 53), in which the elaborate door surround clearly shows its debt to Central American interpretations of the Rococo.

CONTINUING TRADITIONS

There remain two other topics to cover in this gallop through Florida's relationship with classical architecture: the evolution of new community design, and the recent return of building in traditional styles.

The modern history of Florida is a history of new communities—intentional settlements in places that did not necessarily present the organic city-birthing imperatives of trade routes, waterway landings, or rail intersections. In Florida, most new settlements have sought opportunity in unremarkable (and sometimes barely existing) places. Also different is that some had distinctly utopian aspirations.

St. Augustine's history is intertwined with the myth of Ponce de Léon's longevity. The founders of Winter

Fig. 6. Aerial view of Celebration, urban plan by Robert A.M. Stern Architects, 1997.

Fig. 7. Aerial view of Seaside, urban plan by Duany Plater-Zyberk & Company, Architects and Town Planners (DPZ), 1979-84.

Park (1880s) imagined a permanent future in the Eden of the South. DeFuniak Springs (1880s) in the Florida Panhandle began as a Chautauqua, the Methodist franchise of adult education and social assembly. The Koreshan Unity (1894), a community that settled on the west coast in Estero, espoused religious and para-scientific beliefs.

Other communities followed, initiated by prominent individuals and promoted by emerging modern marketing techniques. These include Sebring (1912) founded by the Ohio pottery manufacturer George Sebring; Palm Beach, given impetus by Henry Flagler's turn-of-the-century hotels and house, and later, billed as an alternative to the Mediterranean resorts made inaccessible by World War I; Boca Raton (Addison Mizner, 1924); and five garden cities in South Florida: Miami Beach (Carl Fisher), Coral Gables (George Merrick), Miami Springs (Glenn Curtiss), Miami Shores (Hugh Anderson), and Opa-locka (Glenn Curtiss, on an Arabian Nights theme). All of these can trace influences from Progressive Era movements—the City Beautiful and the Garden City. It should be noted that the land for Miami Beach was created by dredging and filling, while Coral Gables sought to make waterfront by blasting canals. Eventually, the boom gave way to the Great Miami Hurricane-induced bust (1926), which was followed

by the Great Depression. When building returned to Florida after World War II, the original idealism of these city plans was largely ignored.

RECENT DECADES

This disregard of original intentions, with the region succumbing to conventional suburbia, lasted until the 1970s. A new direction emerged under the influence of theorists such as Robert Venturi, Jane Jacobs, Vincent Scully, and Colin Rowe. Building designs by architects including Venturi, Rauch & Scott Brown, Robert A.M. Stern, Jaquelin Robertson, and Michael Graves, and the conceptual drawings of Rem Koolhaas and Rob and Léon Krier gave permission to architects to once again learn from their predecessors. Also important were Charles Jencks's publications promoting this new direction as "postmodernism"; Paolo Portoghesi's lusciously illustrated volumes on Palladio, the Renaissance, and the Baroque; and the 1982 traveling exhibition *Paris-Rome-Athens* and its accompanying catalogue of a vast trove of Ecole des Beaux-Arts large-scale reconstruction paintings.[7] At the same time, the historic preservation movement was evolving to include district preservation (among the first to be so designated nationally was the Art Deco District in Miami Beach) and a broader understanding of the importance of the relationship of individual buildings to their urban context.

Photo: Richard Sexton

Fig. 8. Neighborhood green in Rosemary Beach, town planner: DPZ, 1995.

Photo: Thomas Delbeck

Fig. 9. Windsor, town planner: DPZ, 1989.

Those who encountered this ferment in their schooling (my generation) were entranced by the thrill of discovery and the public welcome of the new direction. The architecture program at the University of Miami was fertile ground for new study of Coral Gables (attached to the larger American context in a 1982 Cooper Hewitt Museum exhibition and publication[8]), as well as Key West and the Miami Beach Art Deco District, which were undergoing restoration. The first art historian's documentation of Addison Mizner's work also took place at this time.[9]

University of Miami faculty explored classicism anew in teaching and practice. Some joined the efforts to recreate the beloved walkable communities of Key West and Miami Beach, in the plans, codes, and early buildings of Seaside. There, in the Florida Panhandle, under the guidance of Andres Duany (Duany & Plater-Zyberk Architects), a host of young classicists received the early commissions that set their professional trajectories. Among them were Teofilo Victoria, John Massengale, Robert Orr, Don Cooper, Scott Merrill, Tom Christ, and Melanie Taylor. Ernesto Buch's Palladian Seaside beach pavilion became a literal poster child for vacationing in Florida.

Seaside's developer, Robert Davis, designed the community's small, classical, central-square post office in 1984. He also persuaded Léon Krier to design his first building for construction in 1985. Krier had eschewed practice to focus on theory. He had articulated the principle that houses should not be considered architecture. And he proposed that the classical and the vernacular are two branches of traditional architecture that have assignments—classical architecture should be reserved for monuments, the vernacular deployed for the urban fabric—only to design the exception to both rules. Notwithstanding, Krier's influence on the architects of late twentieth-century Florida is irrefutable. Joining the acolytes who have followed his theories, he proceeded to design a number of buildings in Florida, including the meeting hall in Windsor, and the Jorge M. Perez Architecture Center at the University of Miami School of Architecture (fig. 10).

With Seaside, the relationship of design and policy became clear (fig. 7). An aesthetically unified place, the growing town modeled a more environmentally responsible and less vehicle-dependent future, enabling thousands of visitors to experience an alternative to suburban sprawl. Its geometrically defined and symmetrical public spaces, compact and disciplined building placements, and front porches shading and ventilating interiors show that the traditions of place-based design, including the original materials and methods of the location (dubbed "the inaugural condition" by University of Miami faculty), when aggregated, can enhance a sense of place and shared identity.

Seaside grew in influence, spawning the movement called New Urbanism,[10] and directly informed urban design across the country—and indeed the world. New Urban communities have provided traditional and classical architecture a dignified venue for placemaking and a role in community building, and an amplified influence beyond the heretofore isolated individual exemplars of dedicated patrons and designers. The architects of these new communities (and in existing historical ones, too) reveled in their regional origins, as their building designs engaged in a place-based conversation about materials, techniques, and details. From the early resorts to primary-home communities with a full complement of uses, to the rebuilding of existing urban neighborhoods, the power of aggregation and of style as unifying identity, grew.[11]

Meanwhile in Florida, an unparalleled array of communities continued to emerge, including Windsor, Rosemary Beach, Watercolor, Alys Beach, Winthrop (figs. 8, 9), and others. Of particular significance are two in Central Florida—Celebration (1997) and Baldwin Park (1997)—representing a coming-of-age for these ideas (fig. 6). Celebration marked the embrace and promotion of the ideals by corporate America, by none other than the Walt Disney Company. And Baldwin Park, a naval air base redeveloped through a public bidding process and executed by Celebration alumni, reflects early acceptance by governmental institutions. Baldwin Park boasts a recently completed city hall of classical design.

The success of the new traditional urbanism bolstered the reappreciation of Florida's historic settlements. The preservation of historic buildings, neighborhoods, and main streets is accepted practice now, although always at risk in the face of increasing pressure from a speculative real estate market. Coral Gables, still fighting the battle one building at a time, nevertheless stands out as a city committed to preservation and to continuing its traditions even as growth and redevelopment are encouraged. Two recently completed new villages have been added to the 1920s roster of "exotic" styles—Bermuda Village and a Dutch Caribbean Village. And, in the still growing downtown, the powerful policy tool of zoning code incentives has guided several large development projects, designed with explicit reference to the double-square proportional systems of the city's early classical landmarks (fig. 11). The city's architecture review board manual, illustrated with historic drawings, promotes current-day emulation of classical formal principles and traditional construction techniques.[12]

Fig. 10. Jorge M. Perez Architecture Center at the University of Miami School of Architecture, by Léon Krier and Merrill, Pastor & Colgan, with Ferguson Glasgow Schuster Soto (architect of record), 2005.

SUMMARY

In retrospect, the history of classicism in Florida reflects the circumstances of the "inaugural moments" of placemaking, often modest when most of the continental country was already well advanced in city building. The influence of trends and intellectual currents elsewhere certainly can be seen, but often greatly modified by response to the region's climate and hasty methods of speculative development. Notwithstanding, the dedication to building with high ideals for a long future is also evident. The neoclassical has provided a timeless quality of permanence in Florida's civic building, with many examples built even during the Great Depression. And the vernacular interpretations of traditions are well suited for picturesque accommodation of the volatile natural context.

The more benign qualities of that natural context, the landscape and its winter warmth, continue to exert their appeal, as do prospects for opportunity, even while the predicted future threatens the viability of much of the geography. A history of adaptation—land excavation and filling, people coming and going—serves as experience and instruction for that challenge. Our predecessors inspire us by their contributions to elevating the human experience above the difficulties of the time. Their example in pursuit of the classical ideals of beauty and unity deserve to be studied, preserved, and emulated.

Elizabeth Plater-Zyberk is a founding principal of DPZ CoDesign, and Malcolm Matheson Distinguished Professor of Architecture at the University of Miami, where she directs the Master in Urban Design Program. Her practice ranges from building and community designs to zoning codes. She teaches university courses in architecture, urban design, and adaptation to climate change. She is a co-founder of the Congress for the New Urbanism and has served on the U. S. Commission of Fine Arts. Among the awards she has received are the Driehaus Prize for Classical Architecture and the Arthur Ross Award in Community Planning.

Photo: Carlos Domenech, Miami, Florida

Fig. 11. Gables Station, Coral Gables, by Jorge Hernandez, in partnership with Gensler (architect of record), under construction 2020.

Notes

(Epigraph) A. J. Liebling, *The Earl of Louisiana* (Baton Rouge, LA: LSU Press, 2008; originally published 1961), 87.

1. William N. Morgan examines this history in a number of publications, including *Precolumbian Architecture in Eastern North America* (Gainesville, FL: University Press of Florida, 1999) and *Earth Architecture: From Ancient to Modern* (Gainesville, FL: University Press of Florida, 2008).

2. In Palm Beach, the Royal Poinciana; in Miami, the Royal Palm; in Belleair, the Belleview-Biltmore Hotel.

3. See Leslee F. Keys, "Palaces in Paradise: Carrère and Hastings in St. Augustine" (p. 6); Wayne W. Wood, "Henry John Klutho in Jacksonville: From Classical Architecture to the Prairie School" (p. 22); and Bruce Stephenson, "Rollins College and Winter Park: Exemplars of the American Renaissance" (p. 14) in this volume.

4. See Wood, "John Henry Klutho in Jacksonville."

5. See Beth Dunlop, "Discovering Addison Mizner: The Elusive Legacy of Palm Beach's Most Important Architect" (p. 30) in this volume.

6. See Arva Moore Parks, *George Merrick, Son of the South Wind: Visionary Creator of Coral Gables* (Gainesville, FL: University Press of Florida), 2015.

7. See Marie-Christine Hellmann, Philippe Fraisse, and Annie Jacques, *Paris-Rome-Athens: Travels in Greece by French Architects in the Nineteenth and Twentieth Centuries* (Houston: Museum of Fine Arts, 1982). This publication accompanied a 1982–84 exhibition of the same name that was on view in the United States at the Museum of Fine Arts in Houston and the IBM Gallery of Science and Art in New York.

8. *The Anglo-American Suburb*, Robert Stern and John Massengale (New York: St. Martin's Press, 1982).

9. See Christina Orr-Cahall, *Addison Mizner: Architect of Dreams and Realities* (West Palm Beach, FL: Norton Gallery of Art), 1977. This publication accompanied an exhibition of the same name.

10. The Congress for the New Urbanism was founded in 1992.

11. One example is the ICAA's own publication that delineates standards for Habitat for Humanity houses. See Zane Kathryne Schwaiger, ed., *A Pattern Book for Neighborly Houses: Details and Techniques for Building and Renovating Neighborly Houses* (Pittsburgh, PA: Urban Design Associates; New York: Institute of Classical Architecture & Art, 2007).

12. *Best Practices for Aesthetic Review* by the City of Coral Gables Board of Architects, 2016.

INVENTING AN ARCHITECTURE FOR FLORIDA

Southern Florida contains a wealth of innovative work by architects who adapted classical and vernacular traditions to the region's unique climate and geography. This body of work encapsulates an approach to designing buildings and communities in a context where precedents for modern programs required looking to distant sources. Representative projects by some of southern Florida's founding architects—spanning 1916 through 1965—are included in the pages that follow. (The work of Addison Mizner is the subject of another essay in this issue.) More can be learned about their work by consulting the bibliography on page 99.

Michael Mesko and William Rutledge

Douglas Entrance, Coral Gables, 1926 rendering.

Dyer Federal Building and U.S. Courthouse, 1933,
Paist & Steward, murals by Denman Fink.

FOR PAGES 48-57 PHOTO CREDITS, SEE PAGE 2.

MIAMI

Upper Left. Miami Beach City Hall, 1927, Martin Luther Hampton. **Upper Right.** Dade County Courthouse, 1928, A. Ten Eyck Brown.
Bottom. Old U.S. Post Office and Courthouse, 1917, Kiehnel & Elliott.

Top. Aerial view of Vizcaya, 1914–23, Francis Burrall Hoffman, Paul Chalfin, Diego Suarez.
Lower Left. Casino at Vizcaya. **Lower Right.** El Jardin, 1918, Kiehnel & Elliott.

FOR PAGES 48-57 PHOTO CREDITS, SEE PAGE 2.

Upper Left. Alhambra Entrance, 1923, Denman Fink (city artistic director), Frank Button (landscape), Phineas Paist, Walter DeGarmo.
Middle. Elementary School, 1923, Kiehnel & Elliott. **Lower Left**. Douglas Entrance, 1924, Phineas Paist, Walter DeGarmo, Denman Fink.
Upper Right. Coral Gables City Hall, 1928, Paist & Steward, Denman Fink. **Lower Right.** George Fink Studio, 1925, George Fink.

Biltmore Hotel and Conference Center,
1926, Schultze & Weaver.

Upper Left. De Soto Plaza and Fountain, 1923, Denman Fink, Frank Button, Phineas Paist. **Middle Left.** Venetian Pool, 1924, Denman Fink, Phineas Paist. **Lower Left.** Coral Gables Congregational Church, 1923, Kiehnel & Elliott. **Right (top to bottom).** Coral Gables Villages: French City Village, 1925–26, Mott B. Schmidt. Dutch South African Village, 1926, Marion Sims Wyeth. French Normandy Village, 1926–27, John and Coulton Skinner. Florida Pioneer Village/Colonial Village 1925–26, John Pierson, John and Coulton Skinner,. Chinese Village, 1926–27, Henry Killam Murphy.

FOR PAGES 48-57 PHOTO CREDITS, SEE PAGE 2.

Top. The Breakers, 1926, Schultze & Weaver. **Middle Left.** First Church of Christ, Scientist, West Palm Beach, 1928, Horace Trumbauer.
Middle Right. Palm Beach Town Hall, 1926, Harvey & Clark, John Volk.
Lower Left. 239–247 South County Road, 1928, Maurice Fatio. **Lower Right.** 450 Royal Palm Way, 1962, John Volk.

FOR PAGES 48-57 PHOTO CREDITS, SEE PAGE 2.

Upper Left, Il Palmetto, 1930, Maurice Fatio. **Upper Right.** Society of the Four Arts, King Library, 1936, Maurice Fatio.
Middle Left. Major Alley, 1925, Howard Major. **Middle Right.** Marion Sims Wyeth Home and Studio, Phipps Plaza, 1925, Marion Sims Wyeth.
Bottom. 411–417 Peruvian Avenue, 1925, Howard Major.

FOR PAGES 48-57 PHOTO CREDITS, SEE PAGE 2.

ST. PETERSBURG/NAPLES

Upper and Middle Left. Open Air Post Office, St. Petersburg, 1917, George Stuart. **Upper Right.** Trinity by the Cove Episcopal Church, Naples,
1951, Howard Major. **Bottom:** Museum of Fine Arts, St. Petersburg, 1965, John Volk.

FOR PAGES 48-57 PHOTO CREDITS, SEE PAGE 2.

Top and Middle Left. Cà d'Zan, 1926, Dwight James Baum. **Middle Right.** Sarasota County Courthouse, 1927, Dwight James Baum.
Bottom. The Field Club, 1925–27, David Adler.

FOR PAGES 48-57 PHOTO CREDITS, SEE PAGE 2.

NOTES ON THE LIFE AND WORK OF
CHARLES BARRETT (1956–1996)

ANDRES DUANY

These notes are based on the personal experience of Andres Duany (DPZ), with whom Charles Barrett was professionally associated during the last decade of his life. The notes were vetted by Scott Merrill, with whom Charles associated from time to time, and are supplemented with biographical details from an interview with his mother, Joyce Barrett. They accompany a selection of Charles's drawings that will appear in a forthcoming monograph showing many of the hundreds of items of his work in the DPZ archive.

Charles Barrett grew up amid the dismal architecture of the central California suburbs. His mother, a schoolteacher (his father was a policeman), was immensely supportive of his architectural inclinations from the first to the last. Charles died at age forty of a congenital disease that he knew would kill him. But he was a prodigy, having produced more than most architects living to prolific old age.

There have been child prodigies in music, dance, and theater, but architecture is "an old man's art." Among the very few precocious architects are Schinkel, Lutyens, and Wright. It is extraordinary what Charles accomplished, as those architects had the advantages of practicing within an intact architectural culture and experiencing surroundings of beauty. Charles had raw postwar America to overcome.

Charles's work breaks into three periods. There are the drawings of his youth, an omnivorous search difficult to describe. Receiving an M.Arch at Yale, he was influenced by Louis Kahn. Afterward, he learned classicism within Allan Greenberg's classical Skunk Works in New Haven, which included many who would be among the most accomplished traditionalists. There he explored a virtuoso Baroque, which was the opposite of the austere classicism that was his mature work.

Charles worked with Robert Orr in New Haven and Bob Stern in New York, and then he came to DPZ in Miami for the last ten years of his life. He would from time to time associate with Scott Merrill. In the period with DPZ, Charles produced two kinds of drawings. The majority illustrate the urban projects of the office, which he might not have completely agreed with. These are the hundreds of drawings colored by the equally talented Manuel Fernandez (another man who died young, not too long after Charles). A second set of drawings were his own studies for himself and by himself. These are the ones that will be published in the upcoming monograph.

In 1994, Charles suffered a stroke. The doctor was to withdraw life support, when his mother arrived from California to forbid it. Charles recovered. Ironically, he had lost the ability to draw, and confronted learning again—becoming twice one of the finest hands of his generation, and perhaps of all time. The drawings after his recovery lean slightly. This was gradually corrected.

Toward the end of his life, Charles was achieving a new traditional architecture that, in its agility and austere integrity, synthesized much of Schinkel, Lutyens, and Wright. Did he need more time? Gilly, like Charles, built only a small pavilion, but their extraordinary drawings influenced architecture for a generation.

Charles's passing in 1996 was a great loss to his friends, but it is conceivable that he had completed his work on Earth. He had outgrown his position at DPZ and was packed to move to Washington, D.C.—the great classical city—when he suddenly died, somehow a hero.

Top left: At times, a project was given over entirely to Charles, to develop with his abilities unconstrained by the contribution of others. This is one of several precise drawings for two blocks of housing in Miami Beach.

Bottom left: At DPZ charrettes, Charles's role was to provide character sketches for typical aspects of the urbanity being developed. They would be generic enough to be representative of the whole, but also detailed enough to awe the public. Charles was chided that he was producing the equivalent of propaganda posters. He was of course uncomfortable with architecture in this role, but the effect was nevertheless delivered, as everything he drew was admired, even by the least sophisticated. His eye was never cloying and could "sell" even the most marked austerity, as shown in this street for the Playa Vista charrette in Los Angeles.

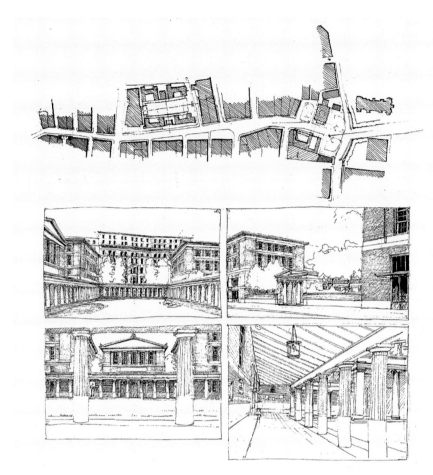

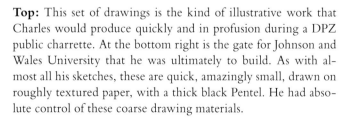

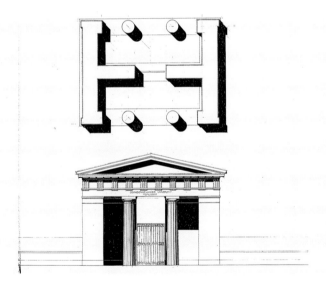

Top: This set of drawings is the kind of illustrative work that Charles would produce quickly and in profusion during a DPZ public charrette. At the bottom right is the gate for Johnson and Wales University that he was ultimately to build. As with almost all his sketches, these are quick, amazingly small, drawn on roughly textured paper, with a thick black Pentel. He had absolute control of these coarse drawing materials.

Bottom left: By his early thirties, Charles had developed an extraordinary facility with all aspects of the classical language. A study sketch like this, with all its complexity, would flow direct-

ly from his mind's eye onto the paper, and without preliminary guidelines. The modeling on this drawing may be compared to advantage with any sketch by Gilly, Lutyens, or Krier.

Bottom right: Charles Barrett and Friedrich Gilly—who also died young—were comparably gifted. Both were able to build only one structure in their lifetime: a temple-front entrance to a court space. Charles's was for the Johnson and Wales University campus in Providence, Rhode Island. It was built exactly as drawn in this miniscule sketch. Early drafts prior to a finished drawing are rare among Charles's papers.

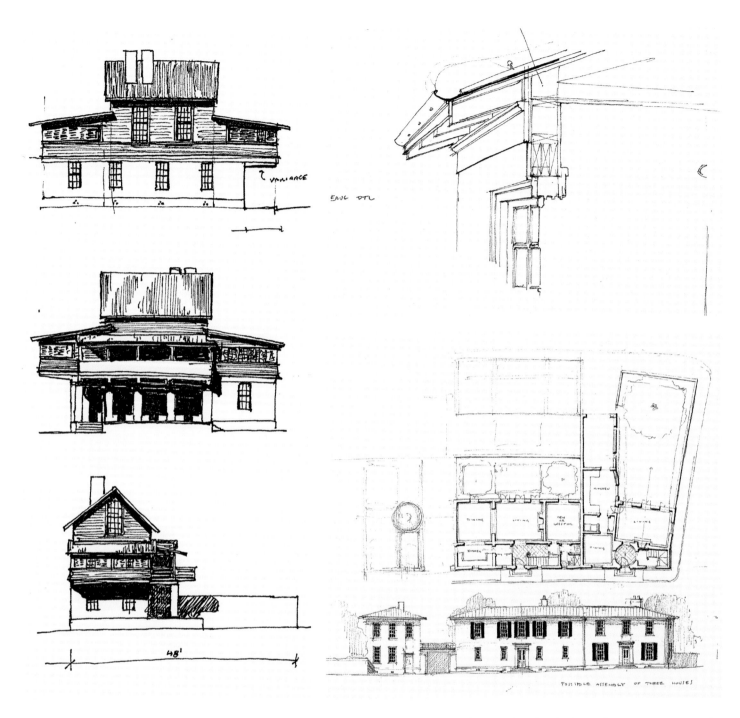

Left: The geographic extent of the DPZ practice drove Charles to engage the vernacular everywhere. This quick sketch for a house in Jamaica does not emulate the vernacular as a style, but displays all aspects of the vernacular mind, including the audacity, the delight, of a raw, untrained architectural talent—the opposite of his own sophistication. His cultural range was enormous. Eventually, it included Germany, Spain, Turkey, and China.

Top right: Charles was a superb practitioner of architecture of all scales, from the urban plan to the detail. Note how in this small sketch, both the construction and the resulting aesthetic are combined—down to the profile of the window muntin. The syntax of the entire building may be derived from this sketch only. His capacity for invention is manifested in the elegant,

unprecedented gutter detail, which combines structure, attachment, flashing, and hydrology in one element.

Bottom right: For the DPZ urban design charrettes, Charles was provided with sites, many of which were purposefully irregular. He would also be provided with the intended building types and asked to develop the ideal into the circumstantial. This he would do, with an uncanny understanding of the imperfection that enlivens the urban fabric, as opposed to the civic building. Notable is the dance of the poche as rooms of ideal geometry celebrate the very slight irregularity of the lot. This drawing, involving even the mullions, was done at a tiny scale showing no more than necessary to illustrate the issue at hand for the Kentlands (Gaithersburg, Maryland) charrette of 1986.

A CONVERSATION IN MIAMI

CLASSICAL IS TRADITIONAL OR . . .

ANDRES DUANY

With so many urgent things to debate today, why get involved in the morass of style?

Alas, it is necessary, because at the academic outposts, the vanguardistas control the discourse—and however much they pretend to a variety of interests, they are all in support of a narrowly focused modernism. For the sake of the students, we must pick up the debate.

The following is a collection of typical arguments that in their sum constitute a defensible position. If you wish to know the Miami position, please read till the end.

I make a distinction among phenotypes of traditional architecture before I make an assessment. There are: (a) The developer's McMansion that spans from Atlanta to San Diego, which is derived from the '70s postmodernism that Krier considers a branch of modernism. We all abhor it, but we cannot ignore it because it is the principal focus of our urge to reform architecture by teaching the correct classicism. The modernist professors present this kitsch to students as current examples of traditional architecture, devastatingly. (b) The correct historicist syntax of, say, Celebration—thanks to UDA's pattern book—that is nevertheless constructed of ersatz materials and is therefore not considered by some of our fundamentalists to be sound traditional architecture. I have no problem with "ersatz." It means "replacement" and, as we know, wood and cast iron have long simulated masonry in many of the best classical buildings. Even Palladio and Nash built with whatever rubble was available under the correct stucco veneer. I think sometimes that those two practical practitioners would have welcomed E.I.F.S. (c) Its opposite, represented by most DPZ towns, which as a result of the code assumes "real" materials, but the language is not "correct." This may be less satisfactory than the ersatz. (d) The tectonically derived architecture of the best of the DPZ towns (Windsor, Rosemary Beach, and Alys Beach), which is not based on a historic style but is driven by the logic of the construction and well-rewarded craftsmanship. This is very good indeed—but expensive. (e) There is also a category that exempts correct and incorrect but derives from certain modernist styles that, despite protestations from all sides, are by now traditional. These can be coded and thus persuaded to participate in urbanism. Among these, the most promising are the Prairie School, the Miesian, and Johnson's International Vintage Style.

Next, is the distinction between style and type. Such things as a townhouse or a porch do not constitute a style. They are architectural types. They perform in useful, socially predictable ways. Types, like courtyard buildings, can be executed in a variety of styles. Porches may be Victorian or Richard Meieresque. (Incidentally one of the earliest buildings at Seaside was a Meiersque house by Tony Ames that met the code perfectly. It can be seen in Mohney and Easterling's book on Seaside.) The vanguardistas accuse porches of being nostalgic. This refusal to discern such an elemental distinction does not betray intellectual coarseness as much as an unwillingness to accept any discipline whatsoever.

In any case, my test for a traditional architecture is not its style but whether the architect is intellectually committed to the reform of our dismal situation. The New Urbanists are reformers while the vanguardistas wish to aestheticize the current debacle. I agree with them that the modern environment is brutal, fragmented, discordant, and a Babel. But, as plenty of the dysfunction is being automatically generated, I don't understand why they should dedicate time and talent to building more of it. Nor do I think that their "critical" stance is effective. Arquitectonica, for example, fifteen years ago, built the largest outlet mall in the world—a brilliant vanguardista design—and no one noticed. It slipped right into the vernacular of kitsch and chaos.

The New Urbanism has a close kinship with the authentic—the original—modernists. Like them, we are committed to reform. Our basic instrument is the efficiency (not just the certainty) available through typology, because we are committed to large-scale effects. Anything important today must be done in quantity. If it is not, it is not important. Everything the vanguardistas do must be unique and, as a result, crafted and personal. So they miss engaging Sigfried Giedeon's "problem of large numbers," which is the authentic modern ethos.

A caveat: the modernism that I refer to, and accept becoming a tradition, is not the recent media-driven psychosis of innovation at all cost. This destroys the possibility of establishing a language. It is this mania for individuality and fashion/style/change that is responsible for the dislike that most people have for modernist architecture. It is not the discomfort and fragility of modernist buildings that causes the problem (some of them are comfortable and durable), but their unintelligibility. No sooner do the common folk "get it" with one architect's work, than the next building comes along, undermining the just-established understanding of the public. I reject architecture as Enigma Machine, changing the transmission code every day.

I do not consider it dishonorable that traditional architecture connects with the common folk, who prefer it. After all, the marketplace is a very sophisticated system of democracy. Those who don't accept the market believe that their knowing better should dictate from their superior position. The vanguardistas are such dictators, but the people resist them and punish them with NIMBYism and trashed buildings. This, while the traditionalists' buildings are bid up to absurd prices (see DPZ or RAMSA). Which group would a rational architect choose to join? I have never envied the martyr-artist, which is the universal product of the architectural academy.

We, the traditionalists of Miami, are students of Vincent Scully, who taught here for seventeen years. We understand and empathize with the many styles of architecture. I will support demolition only when a building is, as the French say, "regrettable." As a practicing architect and one who knows how hard it is to build well, I tolerate the compromised building. I admire those who struggle to build. And I think that those who do not build should not be professors of architecture. Because of the difficulty of building well, traditionalists should be interested in developing an architecture that is tolerant of mediocre workmanship, forgiving of errors, able to adjust to circumstance, including inadequate maintenance—one that doesn't require patrons, in other words. This is not being pessimistic, but a requisite of buildings that must be delivered in quantity in all circumstances. For this reason—like the young Schinkel, Kienze, Aalto, Asplund, Le Corbusier, and Lewerentz—we in Miami have an explicit admiration for peasant and folk buildings and approve of their direct emulation. In fact, when Elizabeth Plater-Zyberk was dean at the School of Architecture, her curricular ideal was "toward plain, old good architecture."

There is another rational reason that would compel me to support traditional architecture today. The components of traditional building constitute an open-shelf prefabricated system: cladding materials, columns, windows, doors, moldings, trim, light fixtures, hardware, gutters, etc., are all compatible, whatever the manufacturer, because they happen to be traditional in form. Modernist architecture of equivalent quality costs much more per unit of area because most everything has to be especially fabricated. The enormous American construction industry is structured this way, and the social disaster that we are attempting to avert will not wait for the reform of the construction industry to become avant-garde. It is ironic, really, that traditionalism is currently prefabricated and available through the net, while modernism must be hand-crafted, with the architect supervising at the shop or on site. Computer-controlled industrial robots are cutting perfect moldings by the mile for David Schwartz, while Steven Holl trowels his carefully flawed stucco by hand. Who is truly the modern architect? (But who is the most ethical is another matter that I avoid.)

My own aesthetically based opinion of a building, and anyone else's, I find boring and inconsequential. An aesthetic opinion is just: you like it and I don't; so what? I am, however, passionately committed to discussing how a building affects a city, because it is verifiable and because it affects our quality of life. A discussion of a building's urban performance need not revolve around style, but there is one condition where it should. Style should be contextual. Urbanists require immersive environments: entirely modernist or entirely traditional both do the job well. I appreciate the new Potsdamer Platz as much as I do Nantucket, although they are incompatible and mutually destructive when in physical proximity. Why is this a concept so difficult to grasp? Most architects (males) have in their closets a traditional blazer with buttons, a sleek microfiber jacket with a zipper, and a utilitarian, bright yellow windbreaker with metal snap fasteners. We know where to wear them. Why not so with buildings?

Urbanists like myself need buildings that have a high degree of harmony (in addition to visual silence). I believe that urbanism requires buildings to be controlled for reasons that include the way that mixed use becomes acceptable when buildings look similar. Style is camouflage that hides radical agendas of diversity. And we also maintain the right of civic buildings to be whatever their architects want them to be, or to freely represent the aspirations of the institutions that they embody. That is a fundamental dialectic of urbanism—one that I have unpacked in the book *Charter of the New Urbanism*, and one that has moved me to write essays in defense of Koolhaas's frightful new Campus Center at IIT. The silent urban fabric as a setting for the expression of the civic building is the fundamental urban dialectic of architectural style.

As an architectural student given only one chance to learn, I would bet on traditional architecture. The win-loss ratio is simply much better. I understand and appreciate the three thousand or so modernist masterpieces as well as anyone (some argue that a rigorous standard would yield no more than three hundred masterpieces). What I can't abide are the concomitant thirty million (or so) modernist buildings of "regrettable" quality that have destroyed the world's cities and spoiled natural landscapes that would have been just fine with traditional buildings. There are so few good modernist buildings that when I ask to visit one, it takes time to think of, and involves some distance to get to it. To find a bad modernist building it is usually possible to stay put and look around. On the other hand, to find a bad traditional building (before 1930) requires research. The win-loss ratio is utterly lopsided. In no other endeavor would such a dismal record be tolerated. A lawyer losing cases at that rate would have no clients, and a doctor would be considered a mass murderer—but architecture is somehow exempt from that sort of assessment. To me, as an urbanist enabling the work of others, I must bet on the likely winner.

I don't think that one or another of the many viable architectural styles is ethically superior, or requiring of greater talent; but I do know that the traditionalists are the heartier folk. They willingly engage in an activity that can be judged. Who is not brave that would step into the arena to be compared to world champions the stature of Lutyens, Schinkel, Plečnik, and Wright? What, in contrast, is so audacious about, say, Eisenman, when he writes his own rules and is the only one who plays by them, and by his own admission throws them out whenever he likes. Of course, he can always declare himself the champ—there are no other contenders in the ring! And so it is with all the vanguardistas: they perform incomparable feats and, if they fall, they declare that such was their intention all along. They are clever cowards no less than the traditionalists are foolhardy in their valor. That is the strongest, the emotional, reason, that I choose to keep company with the architects of tradition.

Andres Duany is a founding principal of DPZ CoDesign. His influence on the practice of planning and urban design is renowned, visible in thriving communities like Seaside, Kentlands, and Poundbury, the new town developed by the Prince of Wales, for which he wrote the design guidelines. His publications include *Suburban Nation: The Rise of Sprawl and the Decline of the American Dream* and *The New Civic Art: Elements of Town Planning*, and he continues work on *Heterodoxia Architectonica*, excerpts of which have been published in the *Classicist*. He is a co-founder of the Congress for the New Urbanism. Among the awards he has received are the Driehaus Prize for Classical Architecture and the Arthur Ross Award in Community Planning.

PROFESSIONAL
PORTFOLIO

Additional images of work in the Professional Portfolio can
be found at classicist.org/portfolios

Tarpon Cove, Palm Beach
Kirchhoff & Associates Architects

Il Cortile, Palm Beach
Fairfax, Sammons & Partners LLC

Photo: de la Guardia Victoria Architects & Urbanists, Inc.

Indian Creek Residence, Miami
Ernesto Buch Architect, Inc., in collaboration with de la Guardia Victoria Architects & Urbanists, Inc.

Photo: Javier R. García Otero

Villa Mare Anna, Punta Cana, Dominican Republic
Ernesto Buch Architect, Inc.

Photo: Jack Gardner Photography

Classical Residence, Upper Grand Lagoon
Eric Watson Architect, P.A.

Photo: Carlos Morales Photography

Ca'Liza, Old Fort Bay, New Providence, The Bahamas
de la Guardia Victoria Architects & Urbanists, Inc.

Coastal Residence, Hobe Sound
G. P. Schafer Architect

Bahamian Compound, Old Fort Bay, New Providence, The Bahamas
Ken Tate Architect

Residence on Lake Worth, Palm Beach
Ferguson & Shamamian Architects

Mediterranean Manor, Palm Beach
Harrison Design

de la Guardia Victoria Architects & Urbanists, Inc.

Dolce Vista, Dunmore Beach Resort, Harbour Island, The Bahamas
de la Guardia Victoria Architects & Urbanists, Inc.

Photo: Nick Johnson

Oceanfront Residence, Windsor, Vero Beach
Clemens Bruns Schaub/Architects & Associates, P.A. and The Associates Studio, LLC

Greenway, Coral Gables
Martinez Alvarez Architecture

Residence, Tampa
Cooper Johnson Smith Peterson – Architects & Town Planners

Photo: Carlos Domenech

Beachfront Residence, Ponte Vedra Beach
Cronk Duch Architecture

Photo: Alan Karchmer

Sago Palm, John's Island, Vero Beach
Moor, Baker & Associates Architects, P.A.

Cottages, Mahogany Bay Village, San Pedro, Belize
Studio Sky

Great House, Mahogany Bay Village, San Pedro, Belize
Studio Sky

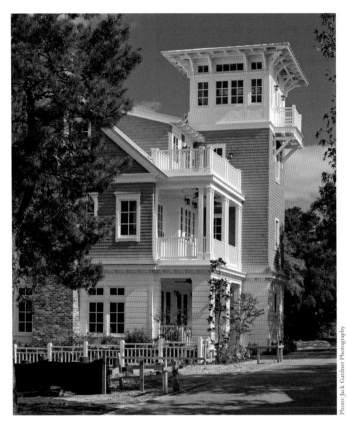

Residences, Seaside
Braulio Casas Architects

Residence, Seaside
Curtis & Windham Architects, Inc.

Photo: Jack Gardner Photography

Residence, Kaiya
Khoury Vogt Architects

Photo: Richard Powers

Ocean Tower, Alys Beach
Michael G. Imber, Architects

Ashford Residence, Alys Beach
Gary Justiss Architect

Residential Block, Alys Beach
Sommer Design Studios

Fonville Press and Sales Center, Alys Beach
Khoury Vogt Architects

The Studio, Freeport
Geoff Chick & Associates

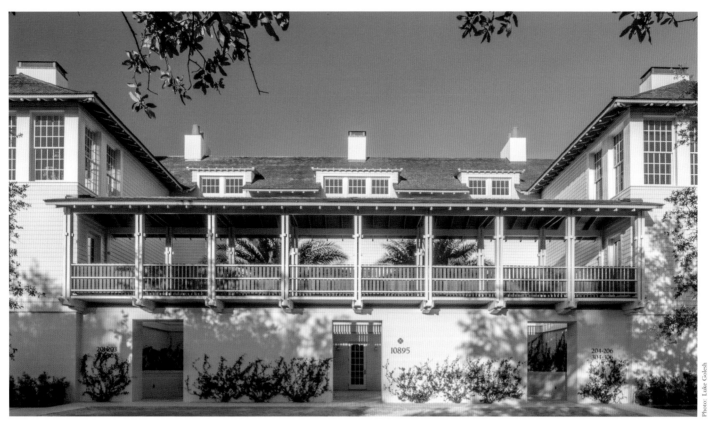

Jungle Trail Condominiums, Windsor
Merrill, Pastor & Colgan Architects

The May, Condominiums and Restaurant, Alys Beach
Merrill, Pastor & Colgan Architects

Photo: Tim Hursley

Chapel of the Holy Cross, Tampa
Duncan G. Stroik Architect, LLC

Photo: Cooper Johnson Smith Peterson – Architects & Town Planners

Corpus Christi Catholic Church, Celebration
Cooper Johnson Smith Peterson – Architects & Town Planners

Heavener Hall, University of Florida, Gainesville
Robert A.M. Stern Architects

Fewell Gallery, Coral Gables Museum, Coral Gables
Jorge L. Hernandez, Architect

Photo: Ray Stanyard

President's House, Florida State University, Tallahassee
Historical Concepts

Photo: George Cott

Academy of the Holy Names, Tampa
Cooper Johnson Smith Peterson – Architects & Town Planners

ACADEMIC
PORTFOLIO

St. Theodore Catholic Church, Flint Hill, Missouri
Daniel J. Prize, 3rd Year Graduate;
Instructor: John W. Stamper

The Grand Madison Hotel, Washington, D.C.
Connor James Kooistra, 5th Year;
Instructor: Julio Cesar Perez Hernandez

Holistic Sustainability: A New High-Speed Rail Terminal, Milwaukee, Wisconsin
Samuel Fischer, 3rd Year Graduate; Instructor: John Mellor

UNIVERSITY OF NOTRE DAME
Notre Dame, Indiana

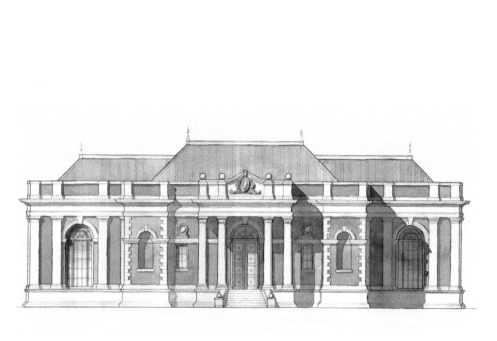

Art Gallery, South Bend, Indiana
Maxwell Meuth, 2nd Year Graduate;
Instructor: Michael Mesko

New Terrace House, Bath, England
Jonathan Roberts, 2nd Year;
Instructor: Michael Mesko

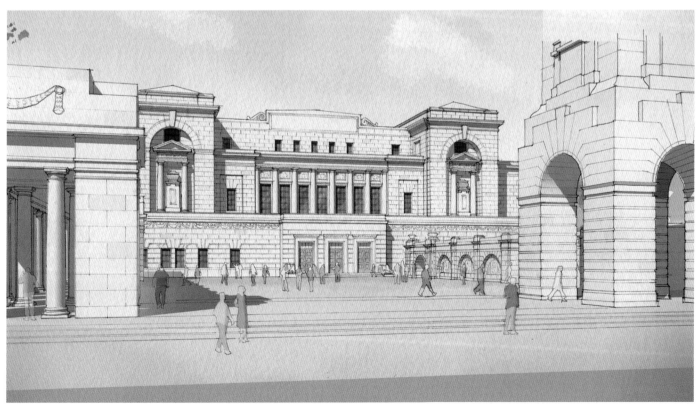

Counter Proposal for the World War I Memorial, Pershing Park, Washington, D.C.
Julian Bell, 2nd Year Graduate; Instructor: Samir Younès

Arabic Hammam, Agadir, Morocco
Joseph M. Faccibene, 4th Year; Instructor: John Onyango

Villa Mati, Mati, Greece
Austin B. Proehl, 5th Year; Instructor: Michael Lykoudis

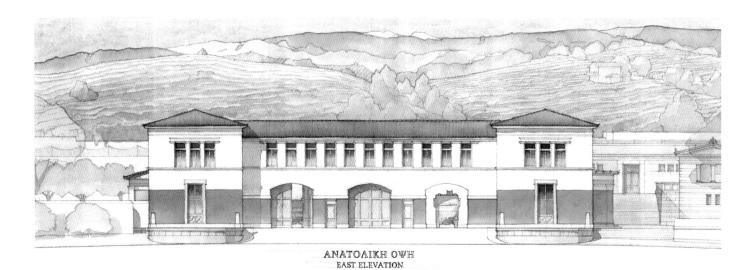

Firehouse, Mati, Greece
Andrew Seago, 5th Year; Instructor: Michael Lykoudis

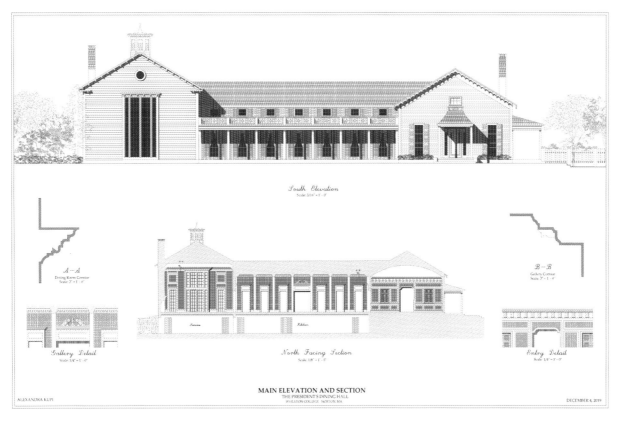

President's Dining Hall and Garden, Wheaton College, Norton, Massachusetts
Alexandra Kupi, 5th Year; Instructors: Oscar Machado and Mark Ferguson

Marsh Harbor Resiliency and Research Center, Marsh Harbor, The Bahamas
Katya Garcia and Cecilia McCammon, 3rd Year; Instructor: David Trautman

Commercial Building, Glasgow, Scotland
Ffion Parry, 1st Year Graduate;
Instructors: Timothy Smith and Jonathan Taylor

Commercial Building, Glasgow, Scotland
Lewis Silburn, 1st Year Graduate;
Instructors: Timothy Smith and Jonathan Taylor

Commercial Building, Glasgow, Scotland
Manraj Bhogal, 1st Year Graduate;
Instructors: Timothy Smith and Jonathan Taylor

Commercial Building, Glasgow, Scotland
Thomas Lockhart, 1st Year Graduate;
Instructors: Timothy Smith and Jonathan Taylor

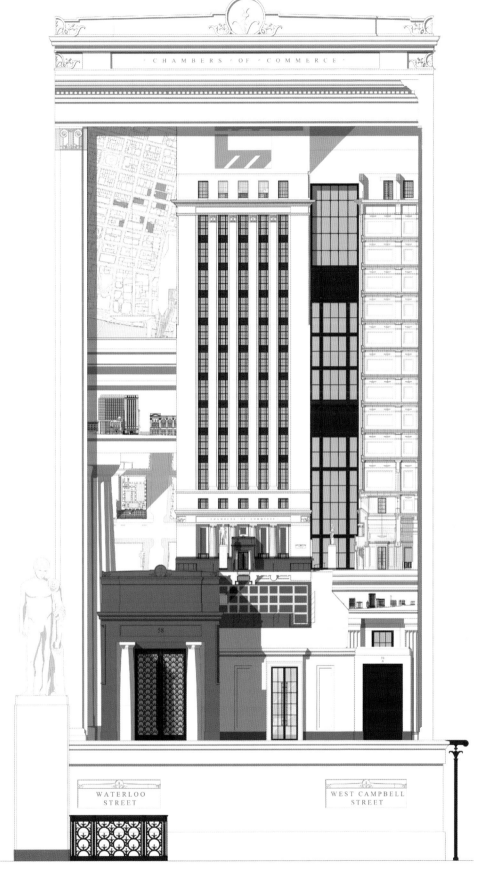

Chambers of Commerce, Glasgow, Scotland
Anthony Anastassios Fitheoglou, 1st Year Graduate; Instructors: Timothy Smith and Jonathan Taylor

American Town and Public Square, Lynchburg, Tennessee
Tommy Vince, 2nd Year Graduate; Instructors: James McCrery and Christopher J. Howard

Single-Family House, Eastern Shore, Chesapeake Bay
Patrick Suarez, 1st Year Graduate; Instructor: James McCrery

Ponte di Mezzo, Pisa, Italy
Jacob Chase, 4th Year; Instructor: James McCrery

CATHOLIC UNIVERSITY OF AMERICA
Washington, D.C.

Arlington Fire Station, Arlington, Virginia
Evan Markley and Sam Merklein, 4th Year: Instructor: Christopher J. Howard

Arlington Fire Station, Arlington, Virginia
Sebastian VanDerbeck and Evan Dziedzic, 4th Year; Instructor: Christopher J. Howard

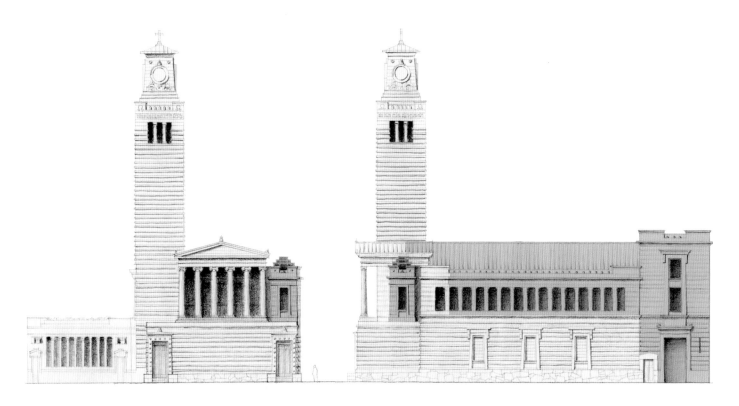

Resurrecting Caledonia Road Church, Glasgow, Scotland
Hamilton R. Brindley, 2nd Year Graduate Thesis; Advisors: Julie Rogers Varland, David Gobel,
Michael Mesko, Christian Sottile

ANDREWS UNIVERSITY
Berrien Springs, Michigan

**New Mixed-Use Building,
Northville, Michigan**
Sara Conner, 3rd Year;
Instructors: Andrew von Maur and Jessica Perry

**Precedent Study,
Eureka, California**
Michaela Broyer, 3rd Year; Instructors:
Andrew von Maur and Jessica Perry

Precedent Study, Bataan, Philippines
Danielle Gonsalves, 3rd Year; Instructors: Andrew von Maur and Jessica Perry

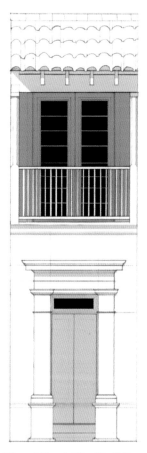

**New Mixed-Use Building,
Arequipa, Peru**
Maryza Eguiluz, 3rd Year;
Instructors: Andrew von Maur
and Jessica Perry

BENEDICTINE COLLEGE
Atchison, Kansas

Tuscan Loggia, Benedictine College, Atchison, Kansas
Jack Edwards; 2nd Year; Instructor: John Haigh

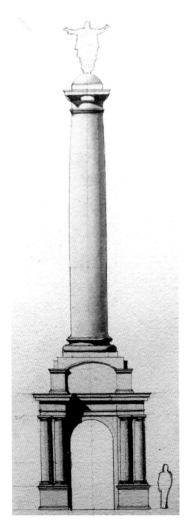

**Sacred Heart Memorial Column,
Benedictine College, Atchison, Kansas**
Ian Reilly, 2nd Year; Instructor: John Haigh

John A. Martin School Main Entrance, Atchison, Kansas
Madison Hemenway, 2nd Year; Instructor: John Haigh

YALE UNIVERSITY
New Haven, Connecticut

TRADITIONAL ARCHITECTURE GROUP
London, England

Study: Palazzo Della Civiltà Italiana, Rome
Jerome Tryon, independent coursework studies;
Instructor: Kyle Dugdale

**Measured Drawing Prize, Historic Facade of
65 Harley Street, London, England**
Jakub Ryng

TRADITIONAL ARCHITECTURE GROUP
London, England

Student Award, Housing in Inverness, Scotland
Aleksandra Zenfa

Park Pavilion, Borlänge, Sweden
Vincent Veneman; Instructors: José Baganha and Paul du Mesnil du Buisson

Apartment Building, Borlänge, Sweden
Michail Sarafidis; Instructors: Allan Struss
and Russell Taylor

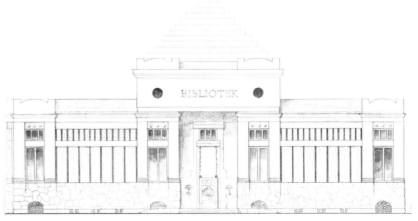

Library, Borlänge, Sweden
Gabriele Vassallo; Instructors: Timothy Smith
and Jonathan Taylor

INSTITUTE OF CLASSICAL ARCHITECTURE & ART

Continuing Education

 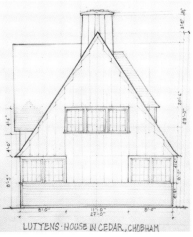 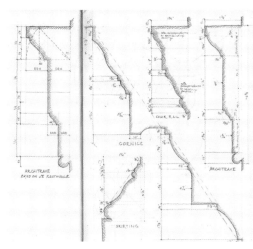

Christopher H. Browne Charleston Drawing Tour
University Workshop

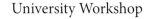

 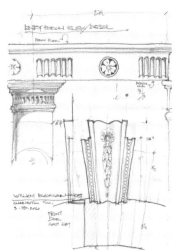  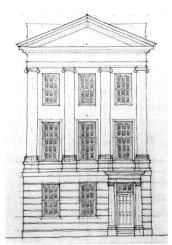

Christopher H. Browne Paris Drawing Tour

(UPPER LEFT) **Watercolor Rendering**, Hanna Propst; Instructor: David Genther; Learning from Lutyens, (UPPER MIDDLE) Jean-Luc Briguet, (UPPER RIGHT) Mark Jackson; Instructor: Stephen Chrisman; Charleston, South Carolina, Studies, (MIDDLE LEFT) **St. Philip's Church**, Patrick Suarez; (MIDDLE) **William Blacklock House** and **Aiken Rhett House,** Kevin Ohlinger; Instructors: Stephen Chrisman, Michael Mesko, Clay Rokicki; University Workshop, (MIDDLE RIGHT) **New Townhouse**, Scott Harrop; Instructors: Clay Rokicki, Jaques Levet, Matt Hayes; Paris, France, Studies (LOWER LEFT) **Bibliothèque Nationale de France (Richelieu)**, Rick Swann; (LOWER MIDDLE) **Bibliothèque Sainte-Geneviève**, Patrick Mahar; (LOWER RIGHT) **Fondation de Coubertin**, Patrick Mahar; Instructors: Kahlil Hamady and Leslie-Jon Vickory

INSTITUTE OF CLASSICAL ARCHITECTURE & ART
Summer Studio in Classical Architecture

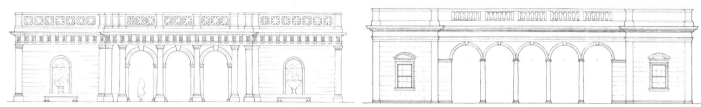

Intensive, New York and San Francisco

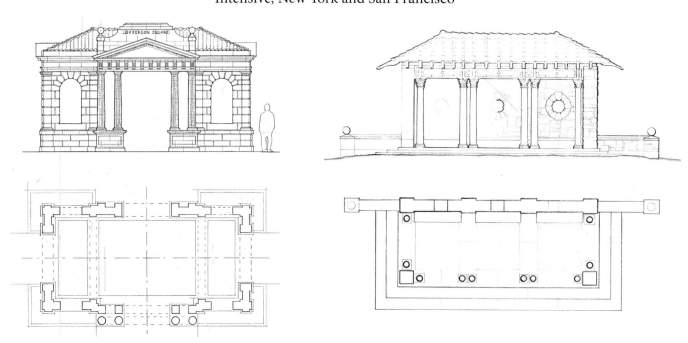

Entry Pavilion, Prospect Park, Brooklyn, New York: (TOP) Evan Markley, Catholic University of America; (MIDDLE LEFT) Sarah Segar, Texas Christian University; (MIDDLE RIGHT) Ian Reilly, Benedictine College; Instructors: Michael Mesko, Mark Santrach, Javier Perez; (LOWER LEFT) **Jefferson Square Pavillion, San Francisco, California:** Patrick Mahar; Instructors: Chris Eiland and Mason Roberts; (LOWER RIGHT) **Pavilion, Prospect Park, Brooklyn, New York:** Tommy Matthews; Instructors: Michael Mesko, Patrick Alles, Chris Eiland

SELECTED BIBLIOGRAPHY

ON FLORIDA ARCHITECTURE

Behar, Roberto, and Maurice Culot, eds. *Coral Gables: An American Garden City.* Paris: Norma Editions, 1997.

Braden, Susan. *The Architecture of Leisure: The Florida Resort Hotels of Henry Flagler and Henry Plant.* Gainesville, FL: University Press of Florida, 2002.

Bramson, Seth. *The Curtiss-Bright Cities: Hialeah, Miami Springs & Opa Locka.* Charleston, SC: The History Press, 2008.

Brooke, Steven. *Miami Beach Deco.* New York: Rizzoli, 2015.

———. *Seaside.* New Orleans: Pelican Publishing Co, 1995.

Broward, Robert. *The Architecture of Henry John Klutho.* Jacksonville, FL: Jacksonville Historical Society, 2003.

Building Through Time: The Making of a School of Architecture, 1926–2001. Miami: University of Miami School of Architecture, 2001.

Ceo, Rocco, and Joanna Lombard. *Historic Landscapes of Florida.* Miami: University of Miami School of Architecture, 2002.

Ceo, Rocco, Joanna Lombard, et al. *Building Eden: The Beginning of Miami-Dade County's Visionary Park System.* Sarasota, FL: Pineapple Press, 2018.

City of Coral Gables Board of Architects. *Best Practices for Aesthetic Review, 2016.* https://evogov.s3.amazonaws.com/media/91/media/44260.pdf.

Curl, Donald W. *Mizner's Florida: American Resort Architecture.* Cambridge, MA: MIT Press, 1987.

Dunlop, Beth. *Addison Mizner: Architect of Fantasy and Romance.* New York: Rizzoli, 2019.

Dunlop, Beth, and Joanna Lombard. *Great Houses of Florida.* New York: Rizzoli, 2013.

Florida Association of the American Institute of Architects, ed. *A Guide to Florida's Historic Architecture.* Gainesville, FL: Library Press at University of Florida Press, 2017.

Florida Atlantic University, ed. *A Guidebook to New Urbanism in Florida (Vol. 1).* Congress for the New Urbanism Florida Chapter, 2002.

Graham, Thomas. *Mr. Flagler's St. Augustine.* Gainesville, FL: University Press of Florida, 2014.

Hoffstot, Barbara, and Arthur Ziegler. *Landmark Architecture of Palm Beach.* Pittsburgh, PA: Ober Park Associates, 1974.

Johnston, Shirley. *Palm Beach Houses.* New York: Rizzoli, 2015 repr.; originally published 1991.

Keys, Leslee. *Hotel Ponce de Leon: The Rise, Fall, and Rebirth of Flagler's Gilded Age Palace.* Gainesville, FL: University Press of Florida, 2015.

Lejeune, Jean-François, and Allan Shulman. *The Making of Miami Beach: 1933–1942: The Architecture of Lawrence Murray Dixon.* Miami Beach., FL: Bass Museum of Art; and New York: Rizzoli, 2000.

Lombard, Joanna. *The Architecture of Duany Plater-Zyberk and Company.* New York: Rizzoli, 2005.

Manucy, Albert. *The Houses of St. Augustine, 1565–1821.* Gainesville, FL: University Press of Florida, 1991.

McClane, Patrick W., and Debra A. McClane. *The Architecture of James Gamble Rogers II in Winter Park, Florida.* Gainesville, FL; University Press of Florida, 2004.

Millas, Aristides., and Ellen Uguccioni. *Coral Gables, Miami Riviera: An Architectural Guide.* Gainesville, FL: University Press of Florida, 2004.

Mizner, Addison. *Florida Architecture of Addison Mizner.* New York: Dover Publications, 1992 repr.; originally published 1928.

Mockler, Kim. *Maurice Fatio: Palm Beach Architect.* New York: Acanthus Press, 2010.

Mohney, David, and Keller Easterling, eds. *Seaside: Making a Town in America.* New York: Princeton Architectural Press, 1991.

Nepomechie, Marilys Rebeca. *Miami, Building Paradise: An Architectural Guide to the Magic City.* Miami: AIA Miami, 2010.

Newcomb, Rexford. *Mediterranean Domestic Architecture in the United States.* New York: Acanthus Press, 1999 repr.; originally published 1928.

Parks, Arva Moore. *George Merrick, Son of the South Wind: Visionary Creator of Coral Gables.* Gainesville, FL: University Press of Florida, 2015.

———. *Miami, the Magic City.* Miami: Community Media, 2008.

Pratt, Theodore. *The Barefoot Mailman, 50th Anniversary Edition.* Hobe Sound, FL: Florida Classics, 1993 repr.; originally published 1943.

Preservation Foundation of Palm Beach, Katherine Jacob, Amanda Skier, and Shellie Labell. *Palm Beach: An Architectural Heritage (Stories in Preservation and Architecture).* New York: Rizzoli, 2018.

Reyher Jackson, Faith. *Pioneer of Tropical Landscape Architecture: William Lyman Phillips in Florida.* Gainesville, FL: University Press of Florida, 1997.

Rybczynski, Witold, Laurie Olin, et al. *Vizcaya: An American Villa and Its Makers.* Philadelphia, PA: University of Pennsylvania Press, 2007.

Scott, Jean, ed. *A Guidebook to New Urbanism in Florida 2005.* Hialeah, FL: Congress for the New Urbanism, Florida Chapter; Dutton Press, 2005.

Seebohm, Caroline. *Boca Rococo.* New York: Clarkson Potter, 2001.

Sexton, Richard. *Rosemary Beach.* New Orleans: Pelican Publishing Company, 2007

Shulman, Allan, Randall Robinson Jr., and James F. Donnelly. *Miami Architecture: An AIA Guide Featuring Downtown, the Beaches, and Coconut Grove.* Gainesville, FL: University Press of Florida, 2010.

St. Aubin Hussey, Susan, ed.; Lillian Jane Volk, Lory Armstrong, Volk, and William Dale Waters, comps. *John L. Volk: Palm Beach Architect.* Palm Beach, FL: The John L. Volk Foundation, 2001.

Thadani, Dhiru. *Visions of Seaside: Foundation/Evolution/Imagination. Built & Unbuilt Architecture.* New York: Rizzoli, 2013.

Waite Romer, Gleason. *Romer's Miami: Windows to the Past.* Miami: Miami-Dade Public Library System, 1985.

GEOFFREY MOUEN

ARCHITECT

535 West End, New York City

LUCIEN | LAGRANGE®
STUDIO

B̈

E. R. BUTLER & CO.

E. Robinson & Co., Boston, Mass.

Enoch Robinson & Henry Whitney (1826)

E. & G.W. Robinson & Co. (1837–1839)

E. Robinson & Co. (1839–1905)

Wm. Hall & Co. (1843–1921)

G.N. Wood & Co. (1905–1914)

John Tein Company (1883–1939)

L.S. Hall & Co. (1914–1918)

W.C. Vaughan Co. (1895–2000)

Ostrander & Eshleman (1921–1992)

Quincy Spindle Mfg. Co. (–1999)

(New England Lock and Hardware Co.)

Edward R. Butler Company (1966–1990)

&

E.R. Butler & Co. (1990–)

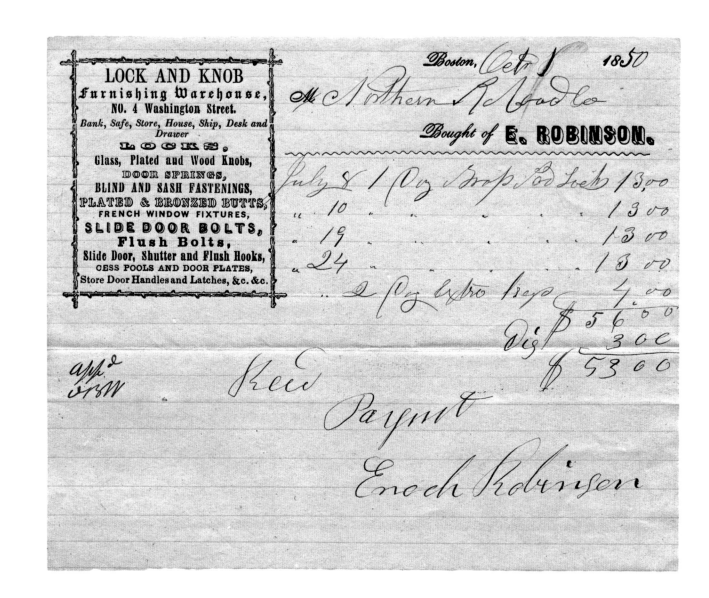

E. ROBINSON & CO., BILLHEAD, 1850

E.R. Butler & Co. Research Library

PETER PENNOYER ARCHITECTS

Rendering: Eero Schultz

— A House in Palm Beach, Florida —

PPAPC.COM

FERGUSON &
SHAMAMIAN
ARCHITECTS, LLP

TELEPHONE: 212-941-8088   www.fergusonshamamian.com

RAMSA
ROBERT A.M. STERN ARCHITECTS

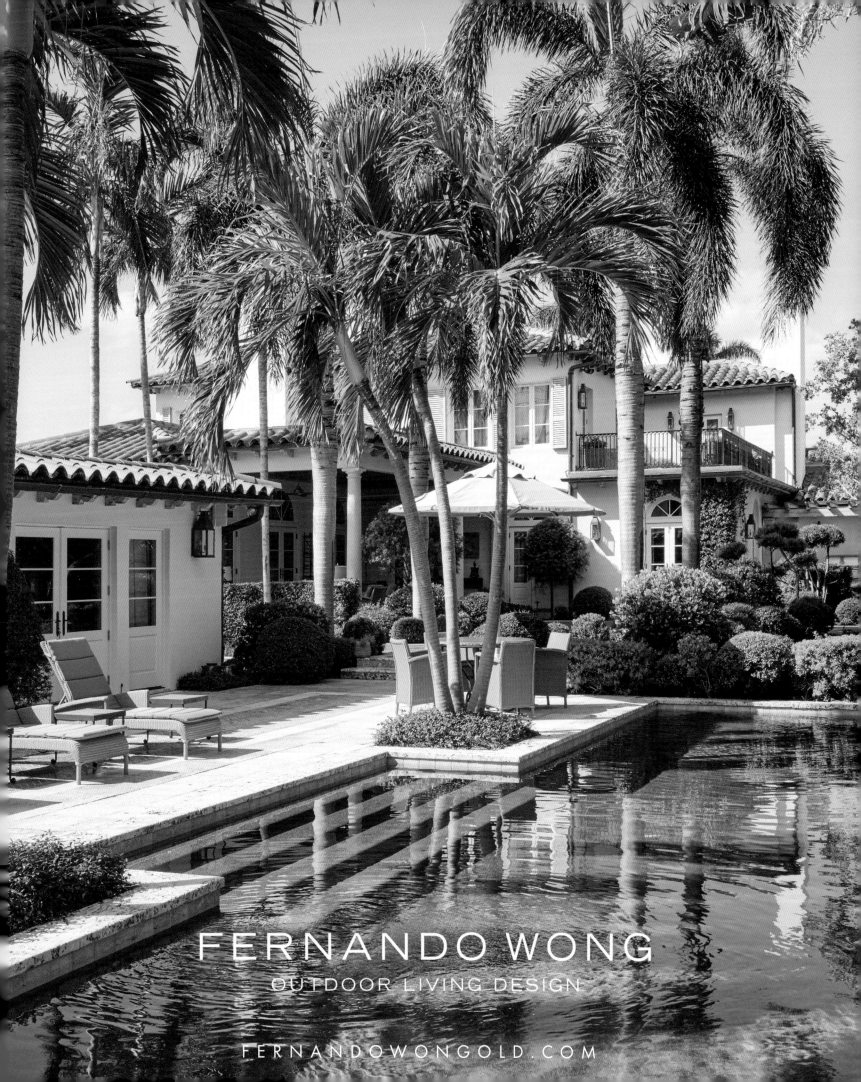

FERNANDO WONG

OUTDOOR LIVING DESIGN

FERNANDOWONGOLD.COM

Project Architect - Jairo Castro, Photography - Durston Saylor

OLIVER COPE · ARCHITECT

135 WEST TWENTY-SIXTH STREET, NEW YORK, NEW YORK 10001

www.olivercope.com   *(212) 727-1225*

DUNCAN MCROBERTS

A S S O C I A T E S

CLASSICAL HOUSES
Architecture, Interiors & Planning

720 MARKET STREET—SUITE G—KIRKLAND—WASHINGTON—98033 TEL. 425-889-6440

INSTAGRAM: @MCROBERTSASSOCIATES — WWW.MCROBERTS-ASSOCIATES.COM — INFO@MCROBERTS-ASSOCIATES.COM

CHADSWORTH INCORPORATED
WWW.COLUMNS.COM

Architect: Mark P. Finlay Architects, AIA; Project: "Palm Beach Residence;" Photography: Kim Sargent Photography

1 800 COLUMNS
T +1 800 486 2118
SALES@COLUMNS.COM

ERIC J. SMITH ARCHITECT

5 UNION SQUARE WEST, THIRD FLOOR, NEW YORK, NY 10003 | 212 334 3993 | WWW.ERICJSMITHARCHITECT.COM

VELLA INTERIORS
BUILDERS OF EXQUISITE RESIDENCES

VELLAINTERIORS.COM ~ 718-729-0026

NEW YORK CITY

Above: Entry for a new residence by Avanzato De

HYDE PARK MOULDINGS

North America's premier resource for custom plaster mouldings.
Offices in New York and Palm Beach.

www.hyde-park.com
tel: 1.631.PLASTER

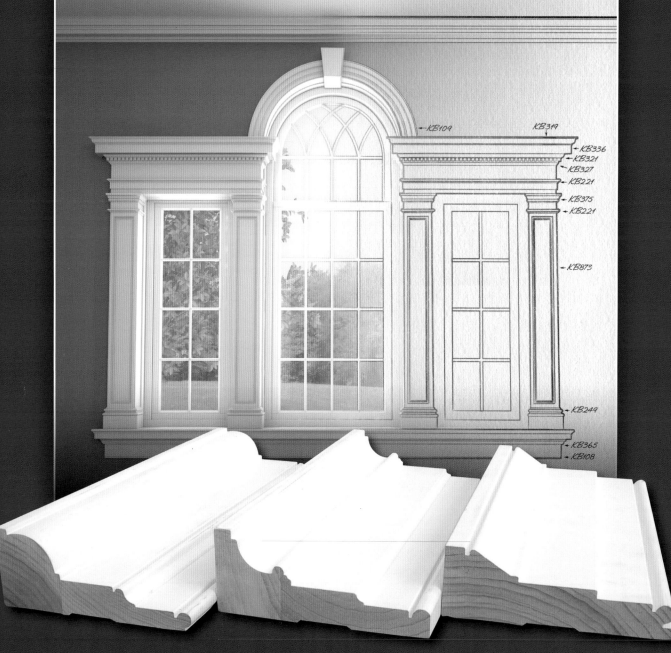

SAFETY, SECURITY, PRESTIGE AND PROTECTION

Distinctive architecture and design enhanced with great craftsmanship and protected with perimeter security that can be integrated into smart home/security technology.

COMPASS
IRON SECURITY

717-442-4500 | GAP, PA
WWW.COMPASSIRONWORKS.COM

PROVIDING ELEGANCE
AND DISTINCTION

Crafted in Lancaster County
with a high caliber of detail and quality in traditional
and contemporary materials and finishes.

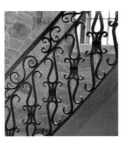

COMPASS
IRONWORKS

717-442-4500 | GAP, PA
WWW.COMPASSIRONWORKS.COM

EXCELLENCE & EXPERTISE
IN ARCHITECTURAL STONE
CORAL STONE-MARBLES-LIMESTONES

MARMOTECH

SANTO DOMINGO, DOMINICAN REPUBLIC

✉ SALES@MARMOTECH.COM.DO

CONTACTS: (786) 797 - 3321   (809) 747-3186

COVAX DESIGN
ORNAMENTAL & ARCHITECTURAL METAL
DESIGN AND FABRICATION

covax-design.com

ARCHITECTURAL RESOURCES
& Associates, Inc.

Custom Entry Door | ARA

Custom Entry Door | ARA

Exclusive Luxury Bathrooms
Handcrafted in England.

C&R

118 Bay Avenue, Huntington Bay, N.Y. 1174
Phone: 631-424-0905, Fax: 631-424-486
E-mail: info@gcmw.com
www.gcmw.com

GOLD COAST METAL WORKS
New York - Olomouc

Interior Design: Victoria Hagan Interiors | Photography: William Waldron

Discriminating clients and design teams turn to Hedrick Brothers Construction for exceptional craftsmanship and uncompromising service. A tradition of excellence is built into the new construction and renovation of world-class residences, condominiums and equestrian estates throughout South Florida. What can we build for you?

HEDRICK BROTHERS CONSTRUCTION

HedrickBrothers.com | #WeAreBuilders

J. J. STONER, Madison, Wis.

1—U. S. Naval Depot.
2—" Custom House.
3—" Barracks.
4—Fort Taylor.
5—Marine Hospital.
6—Sand Batteries.
7—Govt. "
8—U. S. Court House.
9—County Court House and Jail.
10—Catholic Convent.
12—Catholic Church.
13—Episcopal "
14—Baptist "
15—Methodist "
16—" "
17—African M. E. Churches.
18—" Baptist "
19—Public School.
20—Douglas School.
21—Masonic Hall.
22—Odd Fellows Hall.

23—African Masonic Hall.
24—" Odd Fellows Hall.
25—City Hall.
26—Cemetery.
27—International Telegraph Office.
28—John J. Philbrick, Commission Merchant.
29—John J. Philbrick's Wharves and Warehouses.
30—Wm. Curry, General Merchandise.
31—G. W. Ferguson, General Merchandise.
32—John White, General Merchandise.
33—W. D. Cash, Groceries, Provisions and Ship Chandlery.
34—A. Sariol, General Merchandise.
35—Williams & Warren, Furniture Dealers.
36—Fogarty & Johnson, Groceries, Provisions and Ship Chandlery.
37—J. J. Delaney, Clothing, Gents' Furnishing Goods, Boots, Shoes, etc.
38—John McKilip, Boots and Shoes.
39—D. T. Sweeny, Bottler of Mineral Water, Lager Beer, etc.
40—D. T. Sweeny, Saloon and Billiard Parlor.
41—J. H. Gregory's Cigar Manufactories Nos. 10 and 96.

BIRD'S EYE

KEY WE

KEY WES

C.S. MON

188